The Fighting Men of Genesee County, Michigan

Remembering the Sacrifices of Civil War Soldiers from the Flint Area

Scott Roy

A special thanks to Dr. Ami Pflugrad-Jackisch, Dr. Thomas Henthorn and Sarah Stroup for their kindness and ongoing support during this project.

INTRODUCTION

On July 4, 1866, a large crowd gathered in the streets of Detroit to watch the presentation of Civil War flags to the State of Michigan. Henry H. Crapo, a former Flint mayor and recently elected state governor, looked upon thousands of veterans and citizens as he concluded his speech by saying, "Let us, then, tenderly deposit them, as sacred relics, in the archives of our State, there to stand forever, her proudest possession—a revered incentive to liberty and patriotism, and a constant rebuke and terror to oppression and treason."[1] The turmoil and horrors of the Civil War were no longer an actuality, but a memory. The bloodshed was finally over.

The Civil War was truly one of the most pivotal events in the history of the United States. Almost every American citizen has encountered the topic at one point or another, either in school, on television, or from visiting some distant battlefield. However, most residents have failed to grasp one of the most crucial aspects of the subject: how the Civil War affected their own communities. It is unfortunate that while many people are able to rattle off important dates or describe famous historical figures, most of them would be dumbfounded if asked about the contributions of soldiers from their own towns and neighborhoods. For example, in Genesee County, Michigan, many people have overlooked the sacrifices that local soldiers willingly made for their nation and for their loved ones. Therefore, it is crucial to shed light upon these forgotten Civil War soldiers from Genesee County and the roles that they played in shaping the city of Flint and its surrounding communities. Through the examination of various personal accounts including diaries, letters, autobiographies and other memorabilia, this book will relive the war through the eyes of these local veterans. By exploring the lives of these soldiers, their experiences during the war and their roles in the cultural development of Genesee County, Flint-area residents can better understand the heritage of their own locality.

---

[1] Michigan Historical Museum, "Presentation of Civil War Flags to the State, July 4, 1866," *Rally Round the Flags*,
http://www.hal.state.mi.us/mhc/museum/explore/museums/hismus/special/flags/flag1866.html (accessed January 16, 2012).

Currently, there are three main books that provide significant insight into the experiences of Genesee County soldiers during the Civil War. Franklin Ellis's *History of Genesee County, Michigan*, published in 1879, discusses the involvement of Michigan units in various battles. While he focuses in-depth on entire units and their movements throughout the war, his work fails to examine soldiers on an individual level.[2] While Edwin Wood's *History of Genesee County, Michigan: Her People, Industries and Institutions*, published in 1916, contributes to the history of prominent individuals such as Charles Gardner and T. B. W. Stockton, the work is lacking because it does not explain the impact that these veterans had in their communities at war's end.[3] Finally, *Biographical History of Genesee County, Michigan*, published by B. F. Bowen & Co. in 1908, gives a substantial amount of information on a number of prominent citizens from the area. However, this work did not limit its focus solely on Civil War soldiers. While it offered some information on these soldiers, it also offered many biographies of people who were born decades after the war had ended.[4] Essentially, no major scholarly work exists that focuses solely on the history of Genesee County soldiers in the Civil War and their contributions to Flint and its surrounding communities.

Therefore, the main purpose of this publication is to shed light upon the forgotten Civil War soldiers from Genesee County, their wartime experiences, and the significant impact that they had on the cultural development of Flint and its surrounding communities. It allows local residents to tell the story of the Civil War through their own eyes, by using their letters, diaries and memoirs. This publication focuses on the lives of well-known figures such as Stockton and Fenton, but is unique in the fact that it also describes the experiences of dozens of other unfamiliar soldiers from the area. It introduces men like Ziba Graham and George Clute, who have fascinating stories, yet have been overshadowed by other local Civil War figures. It addresses racism and other controversial issues that the Flint area faced during the nineteenth century, and also describes the political impact that the war had on Flint and its surrounding communities. Furthermore, this publication focuses on the influence that the Civil War

---

[2] Franklin Ellis, *History of Genesee County, Michigan* (Philadelphia: Everts & Abbott, 1879).

[3] Edwin O. Wood, *History of Genesee County, Michigan: her People, Industries and Institutions* (Indianapolis: Federal Publishing Company, 1916).

[4] *Biographical History of Genesee County* (Indianapolis: B. F. Bowen & Co., 1908).

had on the development of Genesee County and its culture. It discusses how the Civil War established a sense of self-identity in Genesee County, and illustrates the ways that local organizations are working to keep that pride alive in the twenty-first century. Most importantly, this publication serves as a commemoration of the sacrifices that were made by these brave men, and the importance of honoring them by remembering their stories.

Before discussing prominent individuals from the area, it is crucial to first provide an overview of Genesee County's significance in the Civil War. To an extent, the war's impact on Genesee County was similar to its influence in other parts of Michigan. It led to the expansion of the lumber and other industries throughout the state. It also promoted the development of railroads in Flint and the rest of Michigan, such as the Flint and Pere Marquette Railroad and the Flint and Holly Railroad. Likewise, the war caused a labor shortage in Michigan that resulted in higher wages for workers. Along with most parts of Michigan, Genesee County's population grew enormously just after the war, rising from 22,498 people in 1860 to 33,900 people by 1870.[5]

However, Genesee County's involvement in the war was also unique in several ways. It served as a place of residence for Sarah Edmonds, a female soldier who was the only woman ever fully accepted into the Grand Army of the Republic. It also produced William McCreery, one of the few men to ever escape from Libby Prison. Likewise, the "Flint Union Greys," a Genesee County company in the 2nd Michigan Infantry, contributed an unusually high number of commanders to its regiment, including six field officers, eleven captains and eighteen lieutenants.[6] The war also brought many Flint area politicians into the broader state spotlight, such as William Fenton and William McCreery, who became prominent figures in Michigan partly because of their leadership during the conflict. Therefore, the role that Genesee County played during the Civil War was unique in many aspects.

---

[5] Willis F. Dunbar, *Michigan: A History of the Wolverine State* (Grand Rapids: William B. Eerdmans Publishing Company, 1970), 387 and 405; Albert A. Blum and Dan Geogakas, *Michigan Labor and the Civil War* (Lansing: Michigan Civil War Centennial Observance Commission, 1964), 11-16; Blum and Geogakas, 30.
[6] Wood, *History of Genesee County, Michigan: her People, Industries and Institutions* (Indianapolis: Federal Publishing Company), 340.

ANSWERING THE CALL

After the attack on Fort Sumter on April 12, 1861, Flint and its neighboring communities faithfully answered President Lincoln's call to arms. In fact, by war's end 2,518 residents of Genesee County had enlisted in the Union Army.[7] The county was represented in a multitude of different Michigan regiments. Its citizens enlisted in twenty-three units of infantry, ten units of cavalry and nine batteries of artillery. In addition, a Michigan regiment of engineers and a regiment of sharpshooters contained a substantial number of men from the Flint area. Likewise, many Genesee County residents joined units from other states.[8] While the estimated 2,500 enlistees made up only a small fraction of the Union Army, Genesee County soldiers proved to be both significant and instrumental throughout the course of the war. There is no better way to commemorate these soldiers than by taking the time to remember their sacrifices and learn their stories.

---

[7] *Biographical History of Genesee County* (Indianapolis: B. F. Bowen & Co., 1908), 59.
[8] Ellis, 63.

2nd MICHIGAN INFANTRY

The 2nd Michigan Infantry was organized in the spring of 1861, in response to President Lincoln's call for 75,000 volunteers. Its members originally enlisted for only a three month period. However, after only a short time, the War Department ordered the regiment to be reformed using three year enlistments, and allowed those who had previously enlisted to withdraw their names without penalty.[9] Although the regiment contained men from throughout the state, a significant number of recruits came from the Flint area. Most of these Genesee County soldiers enlisted in Company F, which was referred to as the "Flint Union Greys."

The regiment experienced its first taste of battle during a skirmish at Blackburn's Ford, Virginia, on July 18, 1861. Three days later, it was ordered to cover the Union Army's retreat during the final stages of the First Battle of Bull Run. In 1862, the 2nd Michigan took part in McClellan's Peninsula Campaign, and was engaged in a number of prominent battles, including: Williamsburg, Fair Oaks, White Oak Swamp, Malvern Hill, Second Manassas and Chantilly.[10] That winter, it was present at the Battle of Fredericksburg, but was placed in reserve.[11] In 1863, the 2nd Michigan joined Grant's Army in the Western Theater. It was involved in the siege of Vicksburg, and actively defended the city of Knoxville, Tennessee, during the fall and winter.[12] In 1864, the regiment rejoined the Eastern Theater. That May, it fought at both the Wilderness and Spotsylvania.[13] Later in 1864, it was engaged at Cold Harbor, and was actively involved in the Petersburg Campaign until the close of the war. It mustered out of service on July 28, 1865.[14]

---

[9] *Record of Service of Michigan Volunteers in the Civil War, 1861-1865, 2nd Michigan Infantry* (Kalamazoo, MI: Ihling Bros. & Everard.) 1.
[10] *Record of Service of Michigan Volunteers in the Civil War, 1861-1865, 2nd Michigan Infantry*, 3-7.
[11] *Record of Service of Michigan Volunteers in the Civil War, 1861-1865, 2nd Michigan Infantry*, 8.
[12] *Record of Service of Michigan Volunteers in the Civil War, 1861-1865, 2nd Michigan Infantry*, 8-10.
[13] *Record of Service of Michigan Volunteers in the Civil War, 1861-1865, 2nd Michigan Infantry*, 13-14.
[14] *Record of Service of Michigan Volunteers in the Civil War, 1861-1865, 2nd Michigan Infantry*, 14-16.

Sarah Emma Edmonds

Oh, war, cruel war! Thou dost pierce the soul with untold sorrows, as well as thy bleeding victims with death. How many joyous hopes and bright prospects hast thou blasted; and how many hearts and homes hast thou made desolate![15]

—Sarah Edmonds, 2nd Michigan Infantry

Courage was not limited only to men during the war. Sarah Emma Edmonds, a woman who lived in Genesee County at the beginning of the Civil War, participated in the conflict disguised as a man. Although the exact day is uncertain, she was born in December 1841 in New Brunswick, Canada.[16] She was originally born under the name Sarah Emma Edmondson, but later decided to shorten her name to Edmonds in 1863.[17] After her abusive father announced his plan to marry Edmonds to an elderly neighbor, she fled from her home. Shortly after her escape, Edmonds disguised herself as a male under the name Franklin Thompson and worked as a traveling book salesman.[18] In December 1860 she traveled to Detroit and soon made her way to Flint, Michigan. While living in Flint under the alias Frank Thompson, she first resided on the farm of Charles Pratt. After a few months, Edmonds decided to live directly in town. She rented a room from the pastor of Court Street Methodist Episcopal Church, Thomas J. Joslin.[19]

When the Civil War began in 1861, Edmonds once again took advantage of the alias Frank Thompson and eagerly joined Company F of the 2nd Michigan Volunteer Infantry. Throughout the first portion of the war, she worked primarily as a field nurse and a mail carrier. During that time, Edmonds became very close friends with her comrade Jerome Robbins, a fellow soldier who had learned her true identity. Robbins wrote

---

[15] Sarah Emma Edmonds, *Memoirs of a Soldier, Nurse and Spy: A Woman's Adventures in the Union Army* (DeKalb: Northern Illinois University Press, 1999), 70.
[16] Laura Leedy Gansler, *The Mysterious Private Thompson: The Double Life of Sarah Emma Edmonds, Civil War Soldier* (New York: A Division of Simon & Schuster, Inc., 2005), 1.
[17] Gansler, 180-181.
[18] Although the truth remains uncertain, it is widely accepted that Betsy, Sarah's mother, helped her daughter escape in order to offer her a better life.
[19] Gansler, 19-20.

about Edmonds very frequently in his diary. On one occasion he even praised their friendship by stating, "I often think that no greater blessing at present could be mine than the relief of a friend like Frank, fully appreciating the noble sentiments which the heart should possess and ever ready to justify whatever he thinks can be supported by the right."[20] Although their relationship was often strained, Robbins and Edmonds continued to be good friends even after the war.[21]

Edmonds' first encounter with the horrors of war came at the Battle of First Manassas. During the battle, she provided aid to the wounded. This experience proved to be an eye opener for Edmonds, and she later recalled:

> One case I can never forget. It was that of a poor fellow whose legs were both broken above the knees, and from the knees to the thighs they were literally smashed to fragments. He was dying; but oh, what a death was that. He was insane, perfectly wild, and required two persons to hold him. Inflammation had set in, and was rapidly doing its work; death soon released him, and it was a relief to all present as well as to the poor sufferer.[22]

Edmonds continued to work as a field nurse for nearly a year. However, by the early spring in 1862, she claimed that she wanted to undertake a more dangerous and active role in the Union Army.[23] Although her claims are doubtful and are discredited by most historians, Edmonds asserted that she eventually devoted herself to life as a spy. According to Edmonds, after a Federal undercover agent was captured and executed by the Confederates, she interviewed with General McClellan and filled the vacant position.[24] As a spy, she wore a number of different disguises. On her first mission Edmonds allegedly took on the appearance of a slave, entered the Confederate lines and successfully gathered intelligence about the army and its position.[25] On another occasion, she claimed to have

---

[20] Jerome John Robbins Papers [Microform, Roll 1], Bentley Historical Library, University of Michigan.
[21] Gansler, 219.
[22] Edmonds, 20.
[23] Gansler,
[24] Edmonds, 56-57.

traveled through Confederate territory disguised as an Irish woman named Bridget.[26] Surprisingly, Edmonds abruptly gave up military life in April 1863.[27] According to her memoirs, two events influenced her decision to leave. First, she claimed that she had come down with malaria and needed urgent medical attention. Because Edmonds could not go to a military doctor without her true identity being discovered, she was forced to desert and find a doctor elsewhere. However, Edmonds also admitted that she became weary of military life after a shell exploded near her tent, killing two men instantly and severely wounding four more. After seeing the horrible results of the blast, notably a boy whose arm was torn off and who later died, Edmonds recalled:

> All my soldierly qualities seemed to have fled, and I was again a poor, cowardly, nervous, whining woman; and as if to make up for lost time, and to give vent to my long pent up feelings, I could do nothing but weep hour after hour, until it would seem that my head was literally a fountain of tears and my heart one great burden of sorrow.[28]

After returning to civilian life, Edmonds had her autobiography published in 1864. It was titled *Unsexed, or the Female Soldier*. Because the title was not appealing to many citizens, it was released again the next year as *Memoirs of a Soldier, Nurse and Spy: A Woman's Adventures in the Union Army*. She donated the proceeds of her book to the Christian Commission with the intentions that the donation would be used to care for wounded veterans.[29] In April 1867, Edmonds married Linus Seelye. She gave birth to two sons and a daughter, but all three children died at a young age. In an effort to recover from these tragedies, Edmonds later adopted two boys, Charles and Freddy.[30] In 1884, she was awarded a pension of twelve dollars per month for her military service. Two years later, the government agreed to remove the desertion charge on her record, making her a soldier of good standing.[31] In the years following the Civil

---

[25] Edmonds, 59-65.
[26] Edmonds, 85-98.
[27] Gansler, 172.
[28] Edmonds, 218-219.
[29] Gansler, 184-185.
[30] Gansler, 189.
[31] Gansler, 207-213.

War, Edmonds and her family left Michigan and moved west. After living in Missouri and Kansas, in 1893 they moved south and eventually settled in La Porte, Texas.[32] In 1898, she became the only woman ever accepted into the Grand Army of the Republic. Only months later, Sarah Edmonds died on September 5, 1898, at the age of fifty-six. She was buried in La Porte but was later moved to the G.A.R. plot at Washington Cemetery in Houston, Texas.[33]

Edmonds' greatest flaw was her desire to be remembered by society. Her autobiography strongly hinted that she liked the attention that she was given for being a woman in the Union Army. While the autobiography is extremely interesting to read, Edmond's eagerness to make her story unique and exciting appears to have caused her to exaggerate and even falsify certain portions of her writings. For example, Edmonds wrote vividly about the action at Antietam, yet the 2nd Michigan was never even at the battle. She described the siege of Vicksburg, but had deserted from the army months before the siege took place. Perhaps most skeptical was her recollection of discovering and helping a dying female soldier. While the experience may indeed be valid, it is suspiciously similar to an account that had previously been given by Clara Barton.[34] In fact, it is highly unlikely that Edmonds was ever a spy. Military records did little to support Edmonds in her claim that she was involved in espionage. Although they are entertaining to read about, the adventures that she describes are most likely fictitious.

Whether or not Edmonds' accounts are entirely true will always remain a mystery. However, while she lived in the area for only a short time, there is no question that Edmonds helped instill a sense of pride in Genesee County. After all, Flint was once the home of the only female member of the Grand Army of the Republic. Even though nearly four hundred women served as soldiers during the Civil War, Edmonds' alleged experience as a spy made her story unique. It is this distinction that has made Edmonds into a national hero, and Genesee County was more than willing to claim Edmonds as one of its own residents. Even to this day, Flint makes sure to emphasize the fact that Sarah Edmonds once lived in the town, and there is a historical marker in honor of Edmonds located on the lawn of the Genesee County Courthouse.

---

[32] Gansler, 192; 215.
[33] Gansler, 218-219.
[34] Gansler, 182.

Charles J. Rankin

> Sergeant Howard was also the unfortunate recipient of a disagreeable wound, by the accidental discharge of a pistol. He had been on guard during the day and night of Saturday, and on Sunday morning was cleaning off the rain which had fallen on his pistol the previous night. While doing so, it was accidentally discharged, sending the ball through the large toe of his right foot, shattering the bone below the first joint. He, of course, ridicules the accident, and declares that he will be ready to outmarch any of the boys, as soon as they receive orders to leave, even if it be within a few days.
>
> —Charles J. Rankin, 2nd Michigan Infantry

Charles Jacob Rankin was born in 1839 in Ireland. In 1848, his family immigrated to the United States, where they first settled in Pontiac. After moving to Flint, his father became editor of the *Genesee Whig*, which was later renamed the *Wolverine Citizen*.[35] At the outbreak of the Civil War, Rankin enlisted in the Flint Union Greys of the 2nd Michigan Infantry.

As a soldier, Rankin wrote home very frequently, and many of his letters were published in the *Wolverine Citizen*. He wrote about the health of the soldiers and their daily lives, and also discussed the tediousness of army life. On one occasion, he mentioned a newly formed "Soldier's Debating Club", which had been developed to help combat boredom. According to Rankin, the club was a success and was very influential in, ". . . improving both head and heart."[36] Rankin's writing was not always serious, however, and it often had quite humorous undertones. For instance, in a letter dated June 11, 1861, he described the regiment's rather exciting trip from Cleveland to Pittsburgh, stating:

> Hundreds of beautiful girls showered on the volunteers bouquets, fruit, havelocks, and everything imaginable, conducive to their pleasure and comfort. Kisses were not withheld: and *good looking* men were as a matter of course, the special recipients of these

---

[35] *Biographical History of Genesee County*, 361.
[36] Charles Rankin, "Letter from Arlington," *Wolverine Citizen*, Aug. 24, 1861.

sweet favors. Officers assumed the first prerogative, and, as your readers are aware, Company F not lacking handsome commanders, of course "our boys" received their full share. The Buckeye girls certainly displayed a strong love for the Union and its defenders. They will long be remembered by the Second Regiment.[37]

Rankin's time in the army was short-lived. During the summer, he contracted typhoid fever, and his health steadily deteriorated. On September 20, 1861, Rankin died. In condolences to his family, William McCreery described Rankin as ". . . universally loved and respected by all who knew him." Likewise, William Morse claimed, "His duties he has always performed without a murmur and fully, both as a Soldier and Christian."[38] Rankin's body was returned to Flint and he was buried in Glenwood Cemetery. In a letter to his father only three months before his death, Rankin had written:

> I think that if I fall, you will not be ashamed that a son has died in such a cause. My blood will, I trust, wash out the faults of the past. Should a merciful Providence spare my life, I shall try to return uncontaminated by any evil influences with which I may be surrounded. Aside from that obedience which I owe to a Higher power, my future happiness depends on my returning no worse than when I left. At some future time you will know what I mean. I go prepared, I hope, to meet whatever fate God may have in store for me.[39]

James Bradley

Friend Rankin:—I have noticed in the columns of the *Citizen* communications from Stockton's Independent Regiment; from the Eighth, and in fact from nearly all the Michigan Regiments now in the field. But since the death of your son Charles, very few have appeared from the Second. This is not as it should be. Genesee County is as well represented in the Michigan Second regiment as

---

[37] Rankin, "Letter from Drover's Rest, Maryland," *Wolverine Citizen*, June 22, 1861.
[38] *Wolverine Citizen*, October 5, 1861.
[39] Rankin, "Letter from Fort Wayne," *Wolverine Citizen*, October 5, 1861.

any other now in service. And I can see no reason why we are not entitled to a fair representation in the columns of *our* County paper. Hereafter you may expect to hear from me occasionally, and if I should write anything *you* think would interest your subscribers—anything *worthy* a place in your paper—you are at liberty to publish it.[40]

—James Bradley, 2nd Michigan Infantry

James Bradley was a devoted resident of Vienna Township. He worked as a merchant in the village of Pine Run, which is now the eastern part of the city of Clio.[41] In 1855, he served as School Inspector for the township, and was elected as Township Supervisor in 1860.[42] During the Civil War, Bradley enlisted as a Corporal in the 2nd Michigan Infantry, Company F, on April 23, 1861. He was promoted on a number of occasions, and rose as high as the rank of 1st Lieutenant by December 1862.[43] Bradley's fortunes soon took a turn for the worse, however. While engaged at Petersburg, Virginia, he was mortally wounded on June 17, 1864. He was sent to Armory Square Hospital in Washington, D. C., where he died shortly after receiving his wound. Bradley was originally buried in Arlington National Cemetery. However, his family later had his body moved to Pine Run Cemetery in Clio, where his remains are currently located.[44]

Even after his death, Bradley's sacrifice was not forgotten by Vienna Township. The Grand Army of the Republic Post 194 was named the "James Bradley Post" in his honor. Clio's veterans held meetings there from 1883 until 1912, when the group's declining membership prevented it from meeting any longer. The building still stands on Vienna Road in Clio today, directly across from the entrance of Carter Middle School. It now serves as a private residence.[45]

---

[40] James Bradley, letter in *Wolverine Citizen*, March 1, 1862.
[41] Ellis, 374.
[42] Ellis, 371-372.
[43] *Record of Service of Michigan Volunteers in the Civil War, 1861-1865, 2nd Michigan Infantry*, 39.
[44] Wood, 352.
[45] James T. Lyons, "Another Hall Found," *Newsletter of the Department of Michigan Sons of*

The "James Bradley Post" (author photo)

James Farrand

It seems to me that a new and more stringent policy will have to be adopted by our Government. It is very humane in our Government to allow all these Southern Cities as fast as they come into our hands to fill up with goods and necessaries of life, and so many of their citizens to take the oath of allegiance, not one in twenty of whose motives are honest. They will cut our throats the very first chances, so closely are they united. I say, treat them all as rebels: send them North to provide for themselves; let Uncle Sam provide for his troops while in the enemy's country.[46]

—James Farrand, 2nd Michigan Infantry

James Farrand was a resident of Flint at the outbreak of the Civil War. On April 25, 1861, he enlisted as a 2nd Lieutenant in the 2nd Michigan Infantry, Company F. He was an able soldier, and by August of 1862, he had been promoted to Captain of Company C.[47] As an officer, Farrand was very popular among his men. In fact, his comrade Richard Halsted once wrote, "Lieutenant Farrand is the pet of the Company, and there is no man the Company would obey more cheerfully than him."[48]

Union Veterans, summer 2004, http://www.suvcwmi.org/gar/charters.pdf (accessed April 20, 2012).
[46] James Farrand, Letter in *Wolverine Citizen*, July 26, 1862.
[47] Ellis, 67.
[48] Richard H. Halsted, Letter in *Wolverine Citizen*, March 8, 1862.

Farrand saw extensive action during the war. Most notably, he was wounded at Knoxville, Tennessee, on November 16, 1863.[49]

During the war, Farrand courted a Flint girl named Ellen O. Miles. While on furlough, he returned to Flint and married her on January 11, 1864.[50] After a short time, he returned to his regiment, and was engaged at the Battle of Spotsylvania Court House on May 12, 1864. The commander of the 2nd Michigan, Colonel Humphrey, had been temporarily placed in command of a brigade, and had given Farrand command over the entire regiment. During the battle, a brigade of Confederates under General Wilcox attacked a battery of four cannons belonging to the 19th New York. Defending against the assault proved disastrous for the New York artillerymen, and they were quickly shot down by the Confederates. In an effort to save the artillery from capture, Farrand and some of his comrades in the 2nd Michigan ran up to the battery and started to operate the cannons themselves. The 2nd Michigan successfully drove the Confederates back and prevented the artillery from being captured. However, their victory came with a price. While manning one of the cannons, Farrand had been shot through the head and killed.[51] He was originally buried near the battlefield, but in accordance with his father's wishes, he was later reburied in Green-Wood Cemetery in Brooklyn, New York.[52] Ellen, his wife of only four months, had become a widow by the age of twenty.[53]

---

[49] Robertson, 824.
[50] Flint Genealogical Society, "Genesee County Marriage Index to 1934," http://www.rootsweb.ancestry.com/~mifgs/marriages/faaa-fazz_1.html (accessed May 29, 2012).
[51] Alonzo C. Ide, "Diary of 1864," *United States Civil War Collection at Western Michigan University*, http://quod.lib.umich.edu/c/civilwar1/USCW006.0001.001/1:135?rgn=div1;view=fulltext (accessed May 29, 2012).
[52] Green-Wood Cemetery, "Burial Search," http://www.green-wood.com/burial_results/index.php (accessed May 29, 2012).
[53] "United States Census, 1850," index and images, *FamilySearch* (https://familysearch.org/pal:/MM9.1.1/MF8D-2YH : accessed 29 May 2012), Ellen Miles in household of Nathaniel M Miles, Flint, Genesee, Michigan, United States; citing dwelling 34, family 34, NARA microfilm publication M432, roll 350.

Richard Halsted

The sentinel while on the alert for any moving form, detected something creeping on the ground a short distance from his post. It was evidently neither man nor beast, yet it had the appearance of life. So mustering the courage, with bayonet in hand, he made a gallant charge on Mr. Curiosity, and found it to be a bag of respectable dimensions, filled with some sort of contents, and gliding over the ground like a snake. The bag was full of newspapers, destined for the Rebels, and a long rope was attached to its neck, by means of which a rebel, who had passed the sentry in due form a few minutes before, was engaged in hauling the bag across his beat and down the hill, soon to convey the contents to the enemy in Virginia. The sentry secured the mail, but the Rebel escaped.[54]

—Richard H. Halsted, 2nd Michigan Infantry

Richard H. Halsted was born on October 19, 1838, in New York. He was the son of Joseph Halsted and Elizabeth Carl.[55] Halsted eventually moved from New York to Vienna Township of Clio, and at the age of twenty-three enlisted in the 2nd Michigan Infantry, Co. F, on April 23, 1861. He was later promoted to the ranks of Corporal and Sergeant. Among other battles, Halsted was engaged at Campbell's Station, Tennessee, on November 16, 1863. During the battle, he was captured by the Confederates and was taken prisoner, but was later released and returned to his regiment the following June. Once his enlistment ended, he mustered out of service in July 1864.[56]

After the war, Halsted became active in the local politics of Vienna Township. In 1868, he served as Township Clerk. He also held the position of School Inspector in 1868, 1869 and 1871.[57] At the age of twenty-nine, he married Amanda Halsted, and together they had two

---

[54] Richard Halsted, Letter in *Wolverine Citizen*, March 8, 1862.
[55] Archives of Michigan at Seekingmichigan.org, "Death Records, 1897-1920," www.seekingmichigan.org/discover/death-records (accessed May 31, 2012).
[56] *Record of Service of Michigan Volunteers in the Civil War, 1861-1865, 2nd Michigan Infantry*, 81.
[57] Ellis, 372.

children. While the family resided in Vienna Township, his oldest child, John, died in 1873 at the age of two.[58] Unlike his son, his daughter Ethel reached adulthood. After the war, Halsted remained good friends with his comrade Sarah Edmonds, and they even wrote to each other occasionally. In fact, when Edmonds was appealing to the government for an increase in her pension, she wrote to Halsted asking him to write a testimony on her behalf. Edmond's effort to increase her pension was made in vain, because she died only a year later.[59] In the later years of his life, Halsted moved his family to Concord, Michigan. During that time, he worked as a druggist and a banker, and his daughter was employed as a saleswoman.[60] He died on November 9, 1903, at the age of sixty-five, and is buried in Maple Grove Cemetery in Concord, Michigan.[61]

8th MICHIGAN INFANTRY

The 8th Michigan Infantry mustered into service on September 23, 1861. It was organized at Fort Wayne in Detroit, and was commanded by Colonel William Fenton of Genesee County. The regiment was part of the "Expeditionary Corps" under General William Tecumseh Sherman.[62] In the spring and summer of 1862, it was engaged at Wilmington Island, Georgia, and James Island, South Carolina.[63] In August and September

---

[58] "Michigan, Deaths, 1867-1897," index and images, *FamilySearch* (https://familysearch.org/pal:/MM9.1.1/N36N-6ZG : accessed 31 May 2012), John E. Halsted, 03 Mar 1873.

[59] Clarke Historical Library at Michiganinletters.org, "Sarah Emma Edmonds Seelye," letter from Sarah Edmonds to Richard Halsted, dated September 6, 1897 (Mount Pleasant: Clarke Historical Library, Central Michigan University) http://www.michiganinletters.org/2009/07/sarah-emma-edmonds-seelye_17.html (accessed May 31, 2012).

[60] "United States Census, 1900," index and images, *FamilySearch* (https://familysearch.org/pal:/MM9.1.1/MSM2-6WF : accessed 31 May 2012), Richard H Halsted, ED 3 Concord township Concord village, Jackson, Michigan, United States; citing sheet 1A, family 8, NARA microfilm publication T623, FHL microfilm 1240719.

[61] Archives of Michigan at Seekingmichigan.org, "Death Records, 1897-1920," www.seekingmichigan.org/discover/death-records (accessed May 15, 2012).

[62] *Record of Service of Michigan Volunteers in the Civil War, 1861-1865, 8th Michigan Infantry*, 1.

[63] The battle at James Island is also referred to as the Battle of Secessionville.

1862, it fought at Second Manassas, South Mountain and Antietam. The following year, the 8th Michigan was ordered to the Western Theater, where it participated in the Siege of Vicksburg and aided in the defense of Knoxville, Tennessee. In 1864, the regiment was sent back to Virginia, where it was engaged at the Wilderness, Spotsylvania and Bethesda Church. In the closing stages of the war, it took part in the Petersburg Campaign, and was disbanded on August 3, 1865, at Detroit.[64]

William M. Fenton

"Stand by the Flag. It is the one under which you were born, or named, or obtained protection, and the blessings of a free God, a God of the People."[65]

—William Fenton, 8th Michigan Infantry

The 2nd Michigan was only one of many regiments in which Genesee County men enlisted. For instance, the 8th Michigan Infantry also contained a large number of soldiers from the Flint area, notably its leader Colonel William M. Fenton. Fenton was born on December 19, 1808, in Norwich, New York.[66] After graduating in 1826 from Hamilton College at the head of his class, he spent a number of years at sea as a sailor and merchant before marrying Adelaide Birdsall in April 1835. The couple first settled in Pontiac, Michigan. Then they moved to Genesee County in 1837, where he became active in mercantile, milling and real estate. He became especially interested in legal matters, and in 1842 he began his career as an exceptionally talented lawyer.[67]

Fenton was extremely involved shaping Genesee County even before the Civil War. He was one of the most prominent landowners of the

---

[64] *Record of Service of Michigan Volunteers in the Civil War, 1861-1865, 8th Michigan Infantry*, 1-3.
[65] *Farewell Address of March 1863*, McCreery-Fenton Family Papers [Microform, Roll 1], (Ann Arbor: Bentley Library, University of Michigan).
[66] *Wolverine Citizen*, May 20, 1871.
[67] Fenton Historical Society, "William M. Fenton," http://fentonhistsoc.tripod.com/id77.html (accessed February 15, 2012).

area, and the city of Fenton is even named after him. According to the legend, on August 24, 1837, William Fenton played a card game against another significant landowner, Robert LeRoy. It was decided that the nearby village, previously referred to as Dibbleville, would be renamed in honor of the winner. Fenton won the hand, and the village was named after him. As a consolation prize, the name of the main street in the community was named after LeRoy. The men then continued to play the game, and took turns determining the names of various streets in Fenton, one of which was named after his wife Adelaide.[68] Fenton's love for politics extended beyond the borders of Genesee County, and he unsuccessfully campaigned for the position of State Representative in 1844.[69] In 1846 he became a State Senator, and was later elected as Lieutenant Governor from 1848 to 1852. At the end of his term, he was appointed as the Register of the United States Land Office, and also served as Mayor of Flint for one year.[70]

At the outbreak of the Civil War, Fenton donated five thousand dollars to the State in order to provide equipment for Michigan soldiers. In response to this contribution, he was chosen to be a Major in the 7th Michigan Infantry, but never held the position because Governor Blair offered him the higher rank of Colonel of the 8th Michigan.[71] The regiment consisted of a large number of Genesee County citizens, and the Flint area contributed two companies to the unit: the "Fenton Light Guard" and the "Excelsior Guard."[72] As leader of the regiment, Fenton participated in a number of engagements, some of which included 2nd Manassas, Chantilly, South Mountain, Antietam and Fredericksburg.[73] The war took its toll on Fenton, and his health began to fail. He resigned from the military in March 1863, and in a farewell speech told his soldiers, "My desire and prayers will be for you individually and collectively, that the flag borne by the 8th Mich. will hereafter as it has been heretofore, be borne honorably to the state which sent you forth."[74]

---

[68] "History of Fenton," *City of Fenton Official Website*, http://www.cityoffenton.org/pages/History-Of-Fenton/1 (accessed February 15, 2012).
[69] Fenton Historical Society, "William M. Fenton."
[70] Fenton Historical Society, "William M. Fenton."
[71] Fenton Historical Society, "William M. Fenton."
[72] Ellis, 68-69.
[73] *Diary of William M. Fenton, 8th Michigan Infantry, McCreery-Fenton Family Papers* [Microform, Roll 1], (Ann Arbor: Bentley Historical Library, University of Michigan).

After the Civil War, Fenton's contributions to Genesee County continued. In the years following his military service, he ran for Governor but was unsuccessful.[75] Fenton was one of the founders of the Citizens' National Bank in Flint, and was its first president. He also served as Engineer of the Fire Department in Flint.[76] On the night of November 11, 1871, a fire broke out in the community. As Fenton rushed to the scene of the emergency, he accidentally ran into a post with so much force that it caused internal injury. He died the next day, leaving behind four children. Fenton was buried in Glenwood Cemetery with his wife Adelaide, who had died three years earlier.[77]

Charles Gardner

Charles Howard Gardner was a Flint boy of only thirteen years old when the Civil War began. In 1861, his father joined the 2nd Michigan Infantry and his teacher Samuel (Simon) C. Guild enlisted in the 8th Michigan Infantry. Determined to follow in their footsteps, Gardner begged his mother to enlist, arguing that as a drummer he could take the place of another musician who was old enough to handle a musket.[78] Reluctantly, his mother agreed, and Gardner volunteered as a drummer in the 8th Michigan. After enlisting, he was briefly reunited with his father while their regiments happened to meet in Washington D.C. It was the last time that he saw his father, who died of typhoid fever later in 1861. The following June, Captain Guild was killed in South Carolina at the Battle of James Island.[79] Even after these deaths, Charles Gardner continued to follow his regiment into battle, and his bravery was noted on several occasions. He served throughout the siege of Vicksburg, and was involved in a number of heated battles. Late in 1863, during an engagement at Knoxville, Tennessee, he was tending to the wounded when a stray bullet

---

[74] *Farewell Address of March 1863, McCreery-Fenton Family Papers* [Microform, Roll 1], (Ann Arbor: Bentley Library, University of Michigan).
[75] Fenton Historical Society, "William M. Fenton."
[76] *Wolverine Citizen*, May 20, 1871.
[77] Fenton Historical Society, "William M. Fenton."
[78] Frank Moore, *The Civil War in Song and Story, 1860-1865* (P. F. Collier, Publisher, 1869), 424.
[79] Michigan Department of Natural Resources, "The Drummer Boy—A Poetry Lesson Plan," http://www.michigan.gov/dnr/0,4570,7-153-54463_18670_18793-52914--,00.html (accessed January 8, 2012).

flew through a nearby window, struck him in the shoulder and entered his lung.[80] After receiving the wound, he was rapidly recovering and was expected to live. He was sent back to Detroit to recuperate, and his mother and siblings joyfully awaited his arrival. To their dismay, they were greeted only with news of his passing, as Gardner had died on the way to Michigan.[81] Shortly after Gardner's death, a song was written in his honor by P. De Geer, titled *The Drummer Boy of Vicksburg; or, Let Him Sleep*.[82]

Charles Gardner did not make any major financial or material contributions to Genesee County. Because he died as a child, he had neither the time nor the money needed to make these long-term improvements within the community. However, that does not mean that Gardner should not be held in the same high regards as the soldiers previously mentioned. In fact, the young Gardner made the greatest sacrifice of all to the community: he gave his life. Gardner's story perfectly illustrated the cruelty of war, and made the suffering and hardships caused by war a reality for many Genesee County citizens. Not only did his father and his favorite teacher die, but Gardner himself, only a child, willingly surrendered the many years of life that were still ahead of him in order to make both the community and the nation a better place. While Genesee County remembers prominent veterans such as Fenton and Edmonds, it must also make sure not to lose sight of the young men who never made it home from the war. Gardner represents these men.

David Burns Foote

David Burns Foote was born in Flint in May 1841, and lived in the city of Flint throughout his entire childhood.[83] After Governor Blair's call to arms, Foote felt inclined to render his services to the Union. He enlisted

---

[80] Moore, 425.

[81] Michigan Department of Natural Resources, "The Drummer Boy—A Poetry Lesson Plan."

[82] The Library of Congress: American Memory, "The Drummer Boy of Vicksburg; Or, Let Him Sleep," *America Singing: Nineteenth-Century Song Sheets*, http://memory.loc.gov/cgi-bin/query/S?ammem/amss:@field%28TITLE+@od1%28The+drummer+boy+of+Vicksburg,+or,+Let+him+sleep++By+P++De+Geer++J++H++Johnson,+Stationer,+7+North+Tenth+St++Phila++[n++d+]%29%29 (accessed January 12, 2013).

[83] Samuel C. Guild, "Soldier's Death," *Wolverine Citizen*, Jan. 4, 1862.

in the 8th Michigan Infantry, Co. A, on June 19, 1861.[84] After soldiering for only a few months, he was called upon to give the supreme sacrifice for his nation. While searching for a place to land along the shores of the Coosaw River in Beaufort, South Carolina, the 8th Michigan was suddenly fired upon by a battery of Confederate artillery. At the first shot, a cannonball struck Foote in the head, killing him instantly. The regiment then sailed out of range from the artillery, which prevented any other casualties.[85] According to *History of Genesee County, Michigan* by Franklin Ellis, Foote was credited with being the first member of the 8th Michigan Infantry killed in the Civil War.[86] In a letter of condolences to Foote's father, company commander Samuel C. Guild wrote:

> But our loss like yours is great, almost irreparable, and I cannot express to you the grief which I feel at the loss of one so brave and so good. Burns was beloved by all the company and will be mourned by them long and deeply. Yet it is easier for us to see a comrade fall thus gloriously than to see them waste away by the hand of disease.[87]

Samuel (Simon) C. Guild

I cannot but regret that I am so long delayed from the prosecution of my studies, but this war must be first settled and the majesty of truth and the constitution vindicated; and if I do nothing more in life it will be a sufficient service that I have been a soldier in this war. Yet it is needless for me to conceal my dislike for this kind of life, and my earnest desire is to escape from it upon the first opportunity.[88]

—S. C. Guild, 8th Michigan Infantry

---

[84] Ellis, 76.
[85] Samuel C. Guild, "Soldier's Death," *Wolverine Citizen*, Jan. 4, 1862.
[86] Ellis, 70.
[87] Samuel C. Guild, "Soldier's Death," *Wolverine Citizen*, Jan. 4, 1862.
[88] Samuel C. Guild, Letter in *Wolverine Citizen*, August 16, 1862.

Samuel (Simon) C. Guild was a twenty-two year old school teacher in Flint, who had recently graduated from the University of Michigan.[89] Once the Civil War was underway, he temporarily postponed his duties as a teacher to help in suppressing the rebellion. He enlisted as a Captain in the 8th Michigan Infantry, Co. A, on September 21, 1861.[90] His student, Charlie Gardner, also enlisted in the regiment as a drummer boy. Being the boy's teacher, Guild became especially protective of him, and acted as a father figure for Gardner during their time away from home.[91]

Guild's time in the military was short-lived. On June 16, 1862, he and his companions in the 8th Michigan were ordered to assault Confederate defenses at James Island, South Carolina. During the attack, Guild was wounded. His comrade, George E. Newall, later recalled:

> Capt. Guild was just in the act of firing a musket when he fell. He was wounded in the side. I would have brought him off the field, but, I did not hear the order to retreat; and only became aware our Regiment was retiring, by happening to look around and see the men going off. Alone I could not do it, for I have been a little unwell for a week or so, and having had to double-quick up to the fort, when the fight was over I was so weak that I could hardly get back. He was beloved by all who knew him, and faithful to the last to his country's cause.[92]

Guild died of his wounds that very day; he had mustered into service less than nine months earlier. Two days before his death, he had written a letter to his wife. A portion of it read, "It will be some time ere we can get off from this island, and many of us, doubtless, will not leave it except our spirits. There will be a desperate conflict, but if right and truth conquer what matter *lives*?"[93]

---

[89] Ellis, 150.
[90] Ellis, 76.
[91] John Robertson, Michigan Adjutant-General's Department, *Michigan in the War* (Lansing: W. S. George and Co., 1882), 292.
[92] George E. Newall, letter in *Wolverine Citizen*, July 5, 1862.
[93] Samuel C. Guild, letter in *Wolverine Citizen*, August 16, 1862.

George Edward Newall

> Father, you need not ask me how I felt this time, for I will tell you in very few words. I can sum it all up in a sentence: I never thought of danger until the order was given to retreat; and then I *was* afraid that I might get *shot in the back*.[94]
>
> —George E. Newall, 8th Michigan Infantry

George Edward Newall was born on September 18, 1842. His parents, Thomas and Sarah, were immigrants from England who had settled in Michigan before giving birth to him. In 1855, George and his father developed the firm of Newall & Company, a planing mill which manufactured sashes, doors and blinds.[95] On September 12, 1861, he enlisted in Flint as the 1st Lieutenant of the 8th Michigan Infantry, Company A, which was given the nickname "The Fenton Light Guard" after its commander, Colonel Fenton. He was later promoted to Captain of Company I on September 10, 1862.[96] As a member of the 8th Michigan, Newall served in a number of different engagements. Among other places, he fought at South Mountain, Antietam, Fredericksburg and Chancellorsville.[97] He was also involved in an intense battle at James Island, South Carolina, and later recollected:

> I was on one side of an embankment, and the rebels on the other; and if I had not kept a close and unremitting watch I would surely have been shot. My only chance of escape, in the situation, was to put a shot in the face of every rebel who raised his head above the embankment. This may seem hard to you, but it had to be done, or my life would not have been worth a moment's purchase.[98]

The war took its toll on Newall's physical health, causing him to resign from service in 1863. Only months after his discharge, he married Sarah

---

[94] George E. Newall, letter in *Wolverine Citizen*, July 5, 1862.
[95] Wood, 509.
[96] Ellis, 76.
[97] *Biographical History of Genesee County*, 72.
[98] George E. Newall, letter in *Wolverine Citizen*, July 5, 1862.

H. Freeman, with whom he later had two children: John and Winnie. The couple lived in Genesee County, where he continued to work in the planing mill until 1881.[99] He became a member of the Knights of Honor and the Royal Arcanum, both being societies which focused on providing financial support to the sick and their families.[100] He was also a 2nd Lieutenant in the Flint Union Blues and a commander of the Flint G.A.R. post, Governor Crapo Post No. 145.[101] Newall served as Mayor of Flint in 1883, and also held the position of School Director in Flint.[102] In 1895, he entered into an insurance business with his son John. Newall retired from the business in 1913.[103] After his wife's death in 1897, he was remarried to Julia Hulme Newall. He died a few years later on September 10, 1916, and is buried on his family plot in Glenwood Cemetery.[104]

James C. Willson

It may seem grand and heroic to fight and gain victories, but each one is at an invaluable cost of human life and blood. None but those who are upon the field and witness the missiles of death and destruction flying around in every direction, and see men fall uttering their last grown, while others, mangled and frightfully torn, are calling for some one to kill them that they may be relieved of pain—can realize the misery. Although I prize the professional advantages to me growing out of such an experience, my heart recoils from the sight and I shudder to think I must yet witness more of this horrid barbarity.[105]

—Dr. James C. Willson, 8th Michigan Infantry

---

[99] *Biographical History of Genesee County*, 72.
[100] Ellis, 154-155.
[101] Wood, 673; The Flint Union Blues was a post-war military unit in Flint, which acted in a similar manner as the modern-day National Guard.
[102] Wood, 499; *Biographical History of Genesee County*, 72.
[103] Charles Moore, *History of Michigan* (Chicago: The Lewis Publishing Company, 1915), 1351.
[104] Seekingmichigan.org, "Death Records, 1897-1920," seekingmichigan.org (accessed May 15, 2012).
[105] James C. Willson, letter in *Wolverine Citizen*, June 21, 1862.

James Caldwell Willson was born in Fitzroy, Ontario, on April 28, 1833. As a young man he moved to the United States, where he attended the University of Michigan from 1855 to 1859. After graduating with a degree in medicine, he opened a medical practice in Flint.[106] During the beginning stages of the Civil War, Willson enlisted in the 10th Michigan Infantry. Three months later, on March 3, 1862, he transferred to the 8th Michigan Infantry.[107] As a surgeon in the regiment, he was relied upon to care for the wounded and dying, which often proved to be a daunting task. Regarding a skirmish that took place shortly before the Battle of Antietam, he wrote:

> Our hospital at which were several Surgeons of our Division, with myself, was at a small log house upon the field, and in and around it were some of the enemy's wounded as well as our own. I had just dressed one of their wounded men by the aid of light from a candle, and was removing him to the inside of the house, when *whiss* came a bullet and entered the poor wounded man at his right shoulder, lodging under left scapula. On cutting it out we found it to be from one of their rifles and was evidently intended for one of us. The rascal, whoever he was, fired another which passed through the hat of one of our Assistants, and lodged in the fence close by.[108]

Due to physical disabilities, Willson resigned from military life on March 6, 1863.[109] On May 18, 1865, he married Rhoda M. Crapo, daughter of Governor Henry Crapo. He was elected as the Mayor of Flint in 1879, and from 1881 to 1884 was a member of the Flint Board of Education. In 1884 he ran for the U. S. Congress as a Republican candidate, but was unsuccessful. He was also the Trustee and General Manager of the Michigan School for the Deaf and Dumb, and the Chairman of the Board of Trustees for Hurley Hospital. Willson died in Flint on August 29, 1912.[110] He is buried in Glenwood Cemetery.

---

[106] *Henry Howland Crapo Family Papers*, Finding Aid, Genesee Historical Collections Center at Thompson Library, University of Michigan-Flint, http://www.umflint.edu/library/archives/crapo.htm (accessed May 17, 2012).
[107] Wood, 393.
[108] James C. Willson, letter in *Wolverine Citizen*, October 11, 1862.
[109] Ellis, 76.

Willson was crucial to saving many Union lives, and it is clear through his writing that he was a decent and moral man. However, that is not to say that he was not without flaws. Unfortunately he, like many other citizens of the time, sometimes expressed racially charged sentiments. Occasionally, he would present these opinions in letters that were published in the *Wolverine Citizen*. In a letter published on May 3, 1862, he wrote:

> The negroes show but little disposition to appreciate the efforts of their benefactors: and as freedom is to them synonymous with idleness, impudence, sloth, and vagrancy, and being naturally treacherous and dishonest, they unbridle their passions, and are a nuisance to the Government and to the Army. I think at present we would be glad every one of them were with their Southern masters, however much our feelings of philanthropy may lead us to hope for their freedom, when in the due course of events and time, a colony may be made of them.[111]

While this statement is provoking, it must not be overlooked. It shows that even Genesee County did not escape the discrimination and prejudices of the time. Unfortunately, these beliefs existed right here in our own communities. At times, we tend to disregard them or "sweep them under the rug," but they are a part of our history nonetheless.

Milton M. Fenner

> Ladies, you have been exceedingly kind thus promptly to respond to the wants of our sick soldiers, and as a Regiment I trust we appreciate your attention. You will please accept our thanks and best wishes. I cannot forego a remark in reference to the stock of warm flannels that came in the box from Flint. The sheets, wrappers and drawers will be a luxury to the sick boys. The bed

---

[110] *Henry Howland Crapo Family Papers*, Finding Aid, Genesee Historical Collections Center at Thompson Library, University of Michigan-Flint, http://www.umflint.edu/library/archives/crapo.htm (accessed May 17, 2012).
[111] James C. Willson, letter in *Wolverine Citizen*, May 3, 1862.

ticks, too, are of such excellent proportions! Indeed, I am almost tempted to be sick.[112]

—Milton M. Fenner, 8th Michigan Infantry

Milton M. Fenner was born in Stockton, New York, on July 28th, 1837. During his teenage years he worked primarily as a farmer, but soon took an interest in medicine. After obtaining a medical degree in 1860, he moved to Flint, Michigan, and opened a practice there.[113] Once the Civil War was underway, Fenner closed his practice and enlisted as Hospital Steward of the 8th Michigan Infantry on August 12, 1861.[114] During that time, he was appointed as a war correspondent for two of Michigan's leading newspapers, the *Detroit Tribune* and the *Wolverine Citizen*. Fenner was an able soldier, and by 1862 he had been promoted to 1st Lieutenant for gallant conduct. He was later appointed Assistant Surgeon, and worked as a member of Admiral Dahlgren's staff on the flagship *Philadelphia*. In November 1863, he resigned from military life and returned to New York, where he opened a medical practice in Jamestown. He was later appointed city physician of the town.[115]

After taking up residence in New York, Fenner married Georgia Grandin in 1866. They moved to Fredonia, New York, where he published "People's Dispensary of Medicine and Surgery" and "The Medical Progress." In addition to running his medical practice, he also gave lectures to various medical societies and frequently wrote articles in medical journals. In 1870, he was appointed as a United States Examining Surgeon, and was elected as the President of the Eclectic Medical Society of the State of New York in 1872. He also took an interest in the Dunkirk and Fredonia Railroad, and served as its President, Secretary and Treasurer.[116] In 1878 and 1879, Fenner served as Supervisor of the town

---

[112] Milton M. Fenner, Letter in *Wolverine Citizen*, February 22, 1862.
[113] *The Profile of Milton M. Fenner from the 1881 Atlas of Chautauqua County*, http://app.co.chautauqua.ny.us/hist_struct/Pomfret/Fenner_Milton-Profile.html (accessed June 8, 2012).
[114] Ellis, 76.
[115] *The Profile of Milton M. Fenner from the 1881 Atlas of Chautauqua County*.
[116] *Milton Marion Fenner*, http://www.civilwarsignals.org/brown/signalmen/248/miltonmfenner.pdf (accessed June 8, 2012).

of Pomfret, which was located just south of Fredonia.[117] His wife Georgia died in 1881, and he later remarried Florence E. Bondeson in April 1883. Fenner remained with Florence until his death in on March 14, 1905. He was buried in Forest Hill Cemetery in Fredonia, New York.[118] The M. M. Fenner Hose Co. #2 was named in his honor, and still exists today. It consists of thirty-five men and women from Fredonia and Pomfret, and assists the Fredonia Fire Department in emergency situations.[119]

Charles H. McCreery

Michigan men need not blush at the record of Michigan troops. In the thickest of the battle have they been sent, and not a man faltered.[120]

—Charles H. McCreery, 8th Michigan Infantry

Charles H. McCreery was born in Mount Morris, New York, on February 23, 1838. He was the son of Reuben McCreery and Susan Barker. His older brother, William B. McCreery, became the Colonel of the 21st Michigan and the son-in-law of William Fenton. When Charles was only one year old, his parents moved the family to Flint, Michigan, where he resided throughout his youth. He attended Flint High School, and graduated from the University of Michigan in 1860.[121] Once the Civil War was underway, Charles McCreery enlisted as a Second Lieutenant in the 8th Michigan Infantry. He was later promoted to First Lieutenant and Adjutant on September 24, 1862.[122] During his service, McCreery was engaged in some of the most gruesome battles of the war. He was at

---

[117] *The Profile of Milton M. Fenner from the 1881 Atlas of Chautauqua County.*
[118] *Milton Marion Fenner.*
[119] *M. M. Fenner Hose Co. #2*, http://www.fredoniafire.org/index_files/Page322.htm (accessed June 8, 2012).
[120] Charles H. McCreery, letter in *Wolverine Citizen*, May 28, 1864.
[121] William G. Cutler, *History of the State of Kansas* (Chicago: A. T. Andreas, 1883), http://www.kancoll.org/books/cutler/labette/labette-co-p21.html (accessed June 14, 2012).
[122] *Record of Service of Michigan Volunteers in the Civil War, 1861-1865, 2nd Michigan Infantry*, 88.

Fredericksburg, but the regiment was held in reserve. He was also at Antietam, and later described:

> About four o'clock in the afternoon we were ordered across the bridge, and formed in line of battle on the brow of a high hill next to the stream. The accurate firing of the enemy's Artillery did good execution among our troops. At the double quick we marched across the ploughed field in front of us, and took cover as best we could along the fence, and around several straw stacks. Partly across another field we advanced amid the whizzing of bullets and the bursting of shells. The brave boys fired as rapidly as they could. A part of the Regiment went up to the hill to the extreme advance, and lay beside the Hawkin's-Zouaves. Everything bid fair for a victory on our side. We were driving them on the right, their Artillery began to slacken its firing, and on the left we appeared to be gaining ground. Suddenly on our left, from a corn field, a fresh Brigade of rebel troops began to pour in a destructive fire of musketry. Gen. Rodman was killed early in the engagement, or probably such a disposition would have been made of our men, as to have driven them back on the left. As it was we were compelled to fall back a little—keeping possession, however, of the bridge.[123]

A few months after the battle, McCreery was promoted to Captain of Company F on March 27, 1863. He was wounded in an assault that took place shortly before the siege of Petersburg. For his display of gallantry during the engagement, he was later promoted to Brevet-Major, U. S. Volunteers. He survived the war, and was discharged on October 7, 1865.[124]

After the war, McCreery attended the Union Theological Seminary in New York City. He graduated in 1868, and moved to Chetopa, Kansas, where he organized the First Presbyterian Church. On November 2, 1869, he married Cornella Brower, and they had four children. After a rather short marriage, Cornella died in November of 1877. Two years later, he married Margaret Scott, and raised a family with her as well.[125] After her

---

[123] Charles H. McCreery, letter in *Wolverine Citizen*, October 4, 1862.
[124] *Record of Service of Michigan Volunteers in the Civil War, 1861-1865, 2nd Michigan Infantry*, 88.
[125] William G. Cutler, *History of the State of Kansas*.

death in 1887, he married for a third time in 1889, this time to Mary Pinkerton. They moved to Minnesota, but he later ended up in Washington, where he was located at the time of his death. He died on February 8, 1929, and was buried in Tacoma, Washington.[126]

John Willett

I deeply sympathize with those loyal persons who have lost near and dear friends in this war, and are therefore tired of it and are asking for peace. I, too, have a son who was made a cripple for life, and still another one, tender in years, who fell upon the bloody field of battle wounded, and was carried away by the rebels to suffer starvation and privation of every kind that a malicious foe could invent, in some loathsome prison I know not where. While these things are painful and heart rending in the extreme, yet true patriotism, love of country, love of nationality, and the future good of unborn millions cry aloud everywhere to cease not our struggle nor falter by the way until this fair land of liberty shall be rescued from the hand of the destroyer.[127]

—John Willett, 8th Michigan Infantry

John Willett was born in New Jersey during the early nineteenth century. While his headstone indicates that he was born in 1816, both census records and *Early History of Michigan* by Stephen Bingham suggest that he was born in 1820.[128] During Willett's childhood, his parents moved to Livingston County, New York, where he attended school for several years. As an adult, he served as a teacher for three years, before deciding to pursue a medical degree. After graduating from Geneva

---

[126] Familysearch.org, "Washington, Death Certificates, 1907-1960," https://familysearch.org/pal:/MM9.1.1/N35S-5LG (accessed June 14, 2012).
[127] John Willett, letter in *Wolverine Citizen*, October 1, 1864.
[128] "United States Census, 1880," index and images, *FamilySearch* (https://familysearch.org/pal:/MM9.1.1/MWS7-J58 : accessed 19 Jan 2013), John Willett in household of Geo. W. Oakes, Flint, Genesee, Michigan, United States; citing sheet 167A, family 2, NARA microfilm publication T9-0579; Stephen D. Bingham, *Early History of Michigan* (Lansing: Thorp and Godfrey Printers and Binders, 1888), 695.

Medical College in 1846, he moved to Flint, Michigan, and established a practice there.[129]

In 1862, Willett gave up his medical practice and enlisted as Assistant Surgeon of the 8th Michigan Infantry. As a soldier, he followed the regiment through a number of bloody battles, such as engagements at the Wilderness and Spotsylvania. He also witnessed the explosion at Petersburg, and later wrote:

> Never before was there a more beautiful yet fearfully grand and stupendous scene than now breaks forth to view. Huge bodies of the solid earth were removed from their old and long resting place, and hurled high in the heavens, while at the very same moment hundreds of pieces of artillery opened their noisy mouths and belched forth their missiles of death and destruction upon the terrified enemy, and upon their works of defense upon each side of the exploded fort.[130]

In the fall of 1864, Willett was transferred to the 30th Michigan Infantry, and stayed with the unit for the remainder of the war. After returning home, he became a druggist and was involved in politics. He was elected Alderman of Flint in 1870, and was elected as a representative in the State Legislature in both 1876 and 1878. He also served as the Chairman of the Committee on Asylums for the Insane, and was a member of the Genesee County Medical Association.[131]

Willett married Jane Kuykendall, and they had four children: Frank, Leverett, John and Vienna.[132] Frank, a member of the 8th New York Cavalry, was captured during the war and survived ten months in Andersonville prison.[133] Another of Willett's sons, John, married Rebecca Crapo Durant, who was the sister the well-known William C. Durant and the granddaughter of the former governor Henry Crapo.[134] Willett died in June 1881 and was buried in Glenwood Cemetery.

---

[129] Don C. Henderson, *The Red Book for the Thirtieth Legislature of the State of Michigan* (Lansing: W. S. George & Co., 1879), 573.
[130] John Willett, letter in *Wolverine Citizen*, August 20, 1864.
[131] Henderson, 573-574; Ellis, 58.
[132] Wood, 62.
[133] Ellis, 113.
[134] *Henry Howland Crapo Family Papers*, Genesee Historical Collections Center at Thompson Library, University of Michigan-Flint,

John C. Wolverton

A soldier from Bragg's army, home on furlough, was taken prisoner, and expressing a wish to take the oath of allegiance, the privilege was accorded him. Then wishing to go to his home, a short distance beyond our lines, two guards were sent with him. Proceeding a short distance, he snatched a gun from one, and felling him to the earth, tried to escape. He was captured, tried, sentenced, and hung, within one hour. This, I hope, will serve as a warning to all who may wish to go and do likewise.[135]

—John C. Wolverton, 8th Michigan Infantry and Signal Corps

John C. Wolverton was born on July 22, 1840, in Tioga County, New York. Being the son of Dennis Wolverton and Susan Dunham, John was the fourth of eleven children. In 1844, his parents moved the family to Grand Blanc, where he resided for the remainder of his youth. As a young man, he attended the University of Michigan in Ann Arbor, but halted his studies after learning about the attack on Fort Sumter.[136] Wolverton returned to Flint, where he enlisted as a Sergeant in the 8th Michigan Infantry on September 23, 1861, at the age of 21.[137] He served in the regiment for two years, but was later transferred to the Signal Corps in October 1863. During his service, Wolverton was wounded three times. While at Bluffton, South Carolina, he was shot in the leg. He was again wounded at Black Creek Florida, this time receiving a bullet in the neck. The third wound was received during a battle near Olustee, Florida, where Wolverton's horse was shot out from under him.[138] When recalling the events of that day, Wolverton later wrote:

---

http://www.umflint.edu/library/archives/crapo.htm (accessed May 17, 2012); William C. Durant was the founder of General Motors.
[135] John C. Wolverton, Letter in *Wolverine Citizen*, March 12, 1864.
[136] Ellis, 353-354.
[137] *Record of Service of Michigan Volunteers in the Civil War, 1861-1865, 8th Michigan Infantry*, 146.
[138] Ellis, 354.

On the 10th, while crossing the upper waters of the St. Mary's River, we were fired on by the rebels in ambush, and seventeen were killed and wounded. Being with the advance, one unlucky shot took effect on my horse; and being at full speed, I came to the ground, fracturing my left arm. This accident at this time disappoints me much, as I anticipate something decidedly brilliant before the campaign is over.[139]

Wolverton remained in the Signal Corps until war's end. After the war, he moved to Burton, Michigan, and took up farming. In 1867, he married Frances E. Mason and had two children with her. He was later elected as the superintendent of schools in Burton, and served as the treasurer and supervisor of Burton Township.[140] Unfortunately, Wolverton's status as a generous and respectable citizen did not make him immune to tragedy. On December 22, 1873, his mother, Susan, was working in the house when a nearby candle caught her dress on fire. She received severe burns, and died the following morning.[141] Like his mother, Wolverton's life was cut short. He died on August 21, 1887, at the age of forty-seven.[142] He was survived by his wife, Frances, who lived until 1915. The Wolverton family was buried in Evergreen Cemetery in Grand Blanc.

Horatio Belcher

Horatio Belcher was born in Berkshire, New York, in 1819, the son of Joseph and Wealthy Whiting Belcher.[143] He spent his childhood in New York, where he met his future wife Mary Hungerford. Together, they had three children: Irving, Eugene and Gertrude. While Irving and

---

[139] John C. Wolverton, Letter in *Wolverine Citizen*, March 12, 1864.
[140] Ellis, 354.
[141] Ellis, 353.
[142] Flint Genealogical Society, "Genesee County Death Index," http://www.rootsweb.ancestry.com/~mifgs/rbindex/wint-wooc_1.html (accessed June 27, 2012).
[143] Belcher's headstone states that he was born on December 16 between 1816 and 1819. However, enlistment records show that he was forty-two years old when he signed up for the 8th Michigan Infantry in 1861, indicating that he was born in 1819.

Gertrude reached adulthood, their brother Eugene died at the age of one. In the years following their son's death, Belcher and his wife moved to Flint, where they resided at the beginning of the Civil War. They became devout members of Saint Paul's Episcopal Church on Saginaw Street.[144]

Like many of his neighbors, Belcher felt compelled to join the war effort. He entered service as a First Lieutenant in the 8th Michigan Infantry on August 10, 1861, and became Aide-de-Camp on Colonel Fenton's staff.[145] He participated in a number of battles, including Second Manassas, Chantilly, Antietam, South Mountain and Fredericksburg.[146] He was wounded at James Island, South Carolina, on June 16, 1862, and was cited for gallantry by his superior officers. He was also shot in the elbow at Cold Harbor, Virginia, on June 7, 1864. Despite these wounds, Belcher's continued patriotism led him to reenlist for a second term of service in July 1864. This decision proved fatal, as Belcher met his downfall only a month later on August 19, 1864. During an engagement at Weldon Railroad, Belcher was leading the 8th Michigan in a charge when he was dealt the deadly blow.[147] When describing Major Belcher's final moments, one of his comrades later wrote:

> He was wounded while leading his men in the charge which resulted in the complete rout of the enemy: three balls penetrated his person—one through his leg. After he received the first wound he was admonished to get down where he could be out of danger and could get off from the field, but he seemed to care nothing for his wound, or fear and danger, but dragged himself along, still giving orders and cheering the men on, when he was again struck in the right arm: at the same time another ball penetrated his side, inflicting a mortal wound. He died before they could get him off the field.[148]

Despite this very detailed account, the amount of wounds that Belcher received during the battle is questionable. According to both the letter and

---

[144] "Funeral Discourse," *Wolverine Citizen*, September 3, 1864.
[145] *Record of Service of Michigan Volunteers in the Civil War, 1861-1865, 8th Michigan Infantry*, 12.
[146] "Funeral Discourse," *Wolverine Citizen*, September 3, 1864.
[147] The battle at Weldon Railroad is commonly referred to as the Battle of Globe Tavern.
[148] *Wolverine Citizen*, September 17, 1864.

his headstone, he was wounded three times. However, Reverend Birchmore's eulogy, which was printed in the *Wolverine Citizen* on September 3, 1864, attributed Belcher with having received four wounds during the battle. Adding to the confusion, Wells Fox, a surgeon in the 8th Michigan, later wrote about Belcher's death in his book *What I Remember of the Great Rebellion*. In his writings, Fox recalled, "After the rebels were repulsed he was brought to me terribly shot to pieces, bearing five wounds, any of which was sufficient to prove mortal."[149] Nevertheless, it remains clear that Belcher was willing to make the supreme sacrifice for his country. His funeral was held at Saint Paul's Episcopal Church in Flint, and he was buried in Glenwood Cemetery. According to his headstone, he had participated in twenty-eight different battles during his military service.

Horatio was not the only member of the Belcher family whose life was cut short by the war. His son Irving enlisted in the 16th Michigan Infantry and served from the beginning of the Civil War in 1861 until its end in 1865. Shortly before the end of the conflict, Belcher became seriously ill. He survived the war, and rode with the regiment in the Grand Review of the Army in Washington, D. C. However, the four years of fighting had taken a physical toll on Irving, and he was discharged from the military due to physical disability on May 15, 1865. He never saw his hometown of Flint again, as he died only a few months later on his trip to return home.[150] Eugene, Horatio's first son who had died at the age of one, was later removed from New York and interred with his family in Michigan. Horatio's daughter, Gertrude, continued to live in Flint until her death in 1925.[151] In honor of her deceased brother, Gertrude named her son Irving Belcher Bates. He later served in the 35th Michigan Volunteers during the Spanish American War. They are all buried at the family plot in Glenwood Cemetery.

---

[149] Wells B. Fox, *What I Remember of the Great Rebellion* (Lansing: Darius D. Thorp, Printer and Binder, 1892), 149.
[150] Irving was discharged due to disability only one month after Lee's surrender to Grant.
[151] Gertrude married William Rufus Bates.

De Witt Spaulding

> Oh thou Judge of all. have mercy on all who have suffered here oh Christ thou who agonized in the garden have mercy on them may their suffering here in part attone for their sins. of those who cause us such suffering we would say as thou didst. forgive them for they know not what they do.[152]
>
> —De Witt Spaulding (written while imprisoned at Andersonville)

Perhaps one of the most interesting accounts of the Civil War came from De Witt C. Spaulding of the 8th Michigan Infantry. Spaulding was born New York in 1842[153] and moved Genesee County before the outbreak of the Civil War. At the age of 19, he made the decision to join the war effort and enlisted in the 8th Michigan on August 15, 1861, at Flint.[154] As a soldier, Spaulding fought in a number of prominent battles, some of the bloodiest of which included Antietam and Fredericksburg. He and his regiment also participated in the siege of Vicksburg, Mississippi. While these battles proved quite hazardous, Spaulding's most trying moment came on May 6, 1864, at the Battle of the Wilderness. That afternoon, his division was ordered to charge the Confederate lines. However, the Union attack was repulsed and the Federals were forced to fall back. During the retreat, he came upon a wounded lieutenant, whom he tried to help off the field. After realizing that the lieutenant's wound was fatal, Spaulding quickly fled and attempted to reunite with his regiment. The clouds of smoke and thick brush of the forest proved quite detrimental, however, and instead of returning to the 8th Michigan, he accidentally strayed into a group of Confederates. While writing in his diary that night, Spaulding recalled his capture by stating:

> I was almost frightened out of my wits and trembled violently as they ordered me to throw down my arms and approach them at the

---

[152] Diary of De Witt Spaulding, Entry dated July 4, 1864, De Witt Spaulding Papers, Bentley Historical Library, University of Michigan, Ann Arbor, Michigan.
[153] Familysearch.org, "Michigan Marriages, 1868-1925," https://familysearch.org/pal:/MM9.3.1/TH-266-12117-128997-61?cc=1452395 (accessed August 7, 2012).
[154] *Record of Service of Michigan Volunteers in the Civil War, 1861-1865, 8th Michigan Infantry*, 126.

same time brandishing their arms like so many Indians and calling me all manner of names. I had no Idea at the time they intended to spare my life they threatened me so but fortunately a Volley from our army silenced them and probably they thought my fate might be theirs if they murdered me and I was finally conducted to the rear by an Alabamian who treated me in a very civil and Gentlemanlike manner not allowing me to be insulted or any of my clothes taken while with him.[155]

As Spaulding was escorted to the rear, he passed the dying Union General James Wadsworth, who had been shot in the head and was leaning against a tree. He was then placed in a group of Union prisoners, and they were stripped of their clothing and valuables. While traveling to the prison camp, he recalled that the men were fed hard bread and maggot-infested meat.[156]

Eventually, Spaulding and the other Federals were sent to the infamous Andersonville Prison. Upon examining the camp, he was appalled at the number of deprived, dying men that he saw. He also came across a number of friends from Genesee County. Shortly after Spaulding's arrival at Andersonville, an old schoolmate from Fenton arrived named Hiram Whalen.[157] Spaulding was also reunited with another of his friends, Elezar Thatcher of Fenton. Unfortunately, both Whalen and Thatcher, who were members of the 6th Michigan Cavalry, died during their time at the camp.[158] Seeing the suffering of both his friends and his thousands of Union comrades undoubtedly outraged Spaulding. Adding to his misery, less than two months after his capture, he spent the Fourth of July in Andersonville. He reminisced about the meaning behind the holiday, and wrote:

> Here we are in free America supposed to be a model for all nations. and here exists suffering no one can portray helpless and defenseless and while in this state shot down for the most trifling offense Hand cuffed with a 60# [pound] Ball and chain, gagged,

---

[155] Diary of De Witt Spaulding, May 6, 1864.
[156] Diary of De Witt Spaulding, May 6, 1864.
[157] Whalen was a member of the 6th Michigan Cavalry.
[158] Diary of De Witt Spaulding, July 3, 1864.

put in the stock, Beaten, torture of every kind. and on all sides we can hear the cry of give out bread only a small piece of Bread for I am starving I am dying.[159]

However, Spaulding and the Andersonville prisoners faced other enemies besides hunger and disease. One of the most hazardous threats to the inmates came from a group of Union soldiers who were known as "Raiders". Basically, these Raiders were Union prisoners who banded together and attacked other inmates in order to steal their food and possessions. At times, these attacks resulted in murder. Eventually, the Confederate guards gave the prisoners permission to form a police force, which successfully captured the attackers. Shortly after Spaulding's arrival at Andersonville, the Raiders were put on trial. The jurors consisted of a fresh group of prisoners who had just arrived at the camp, and who were considered unbiased because they had not experienced the atrocities of the Raiders firsthand. After being found guilty, the six leaders of the group were sentenced to death. Spaulding witnessed the hanging on July 11, 1864, and was quite moved by it. Pitying the offenders, he wrote:

> The Gallow was erected near the south Gate. at first I thought it was done to give the Prisoners a scare but I found our men was in earnest. when the Prisoners were brought in upon seeing the Scaffold erected one of them made a break to get away but it was of no avail he ran a short distance was captured brought back and five were soon swinging in the air the other having broken his rope. the noose of this unfortunate victim being adjusted again he was soon swinging beside his Associates. the hour for their doom being fixed at half past 4 all but two plead innocent who said nothing some asked all those whom they had wronged to forgive them and at the time fixed they were all launched into eternity.[160]

Less than a year after the Raiders were executed, the Civil War came to an end. Unlike many of his less fortunate comrades, Spaulding

---

[159]Diary of De Witt Spaulding, July 4, 1864.
[160] *Diary of De Witt Spaulding, Entry dated July 11, 1864, De Witt Spaulding Papers* (Ann Arbor: Bentley Historical Library, University of Michigan).

survived his stay at Andersonville Prison. He mustered out of service on July 30, 1865.[161] In 1867, he married Martha (Mattie) B. Clark of Fenton.[162] However, Mattie died in 1871 after only about four years of marriage. She was buried in Oakwood Cemetery of Fenton.[163] Spaulding later remarried Isabella (Belle) Spaulding and moved to Wayne, Michigan. However, he honored his first wife by naming one of his daughters "Mattie" in her memory. In addition to his daughter Mattie, he had two sons with Belle: Ray Spaulding and Dewitt Rose Spaulding. Unfortunately, Dewitt Rose died at the age of eight, but Mattie and Ray reached adulthood.[164] Dewitt C. Spaulding died on May 24, 1926, and is buried at Woodmere Cemetery in Detroit.[165]

10th MICHIGAN INFANTRY

The 10th Michigan Infantry was organized in Flint in February 1862. After being mustered into service, the regiment was sent to Tennessee, where it frequently met Confederate hostility. Most notably, it participated in the battles of Corinth and Stones River. However, it spent most of its time building fortifications, guarding trains, and going on reconnaissance missions, which became its primary function throughout most of 1862.[166] In 1863, the regiment participated in several heated engagements, notably the battles of Chickamauga and Missionary Ridge. In 1864, the 10th Michigan was ordered to Georgia, where it fought in the Battle of Buzzard's Roost on February 25. Later that year, it played an active role in the siege of Atlanta, and was a part of Sherman's "March to

---

[161] *Record of Service of Michigan Volunteers in the Civil War, 1861-1865, 8th Michigan Infantry*, 126.
[162] Familysearch.org, "Michigan Marriages, 1868-1925," https://familysearch.org/pal:/MM9.3.1/TH-266-12117-128997-61?cc=1452395 (accessed August 7, 2012).
[163] "Oakwood Cemetery of Fenton, Genesee County, Tombstone Photographs," *U.S. Gen Web Archives Project*, http://www.usgwarchives.net/mi/tsphoto/genesee/oakwoodfenton/oakwoodfenton_s.htm (accessed August 7, 2012).
[164] Familysearch.org, "Michigan Deaths, 1867-1897," https://familysearch.org/pal:/MM9.1.1/N3F9-2R5 (accessed August 7, 2012).
[165] Woodmere Cemetery, "Woodmere Cemetery Records Database," http://www.woodmerecemeteryresearch.com/records.php (accessed August 7, 2012).
[166] *Record of Service of Michigan Volunteers in the Civil War, 1861-1865, 10th Michigan Infantry*, 1-2.

the Sea." In 1865, the regiment was engaged in a number of skirmishes in the Carolinas. Most notably, it fought fiercely at Bentonville, North Carolina, in March 1865. At the end of the war, 10th Michigan participated in the Grand Review of the Army, and mustered out of service on July 19, 1865.[167]

Corydon E. Foote

The grave of Corydon Foote (author photo)

Many soldiers displayed a considerable amount of heroism without ever even discharging a weapon, as illustrated by the actions of drummer Corydon Edward Foote. Foote was born in Genesee County on January 9, 1849.[168] He lived in the community of Whigville, which is now part of Grand Blanc. Much to the dismay of his parents, Foote enlisted as a drummer in the State militia, which later became the 10th Michigan Infantry. At the time of his enlistment, he was only thirteen years old and was so small that his colonel had to keep him out of sight as the regiment was being mustered into service.[169] Although he never fired a weapon,

---

[167] *Record of Service of Michigan Volunteers in the Civil War, 1861-1865, 10th Michigan Infantry*, 1-2.
[168] "Corydon Foote, Flint's Last Veteran of the Civil War, Succumbs at 95," *Flint Journal*, January 10, 1944.
[169] *Portrait and Biographical Record of Genesee, Lapeer and Tuscola Counties, Michigan* (Chicago: Chapman Bros., 1892), 992; "Corydon Foote, Flint's Last Veteran of the Civil War, Succumbs at 95," *Flint Journal*, January 10, 1944.

Foote's talent as a drummer nonetheless made him a valuable asset to the Union Army. He participated in numerous engagements over the course of the Civil War, notably battles at Corinth, Chickamauga and Missionary Ridge. He also took part in Sherman's infamous "March to the Sea" and frequently wrote home during the campaign.[170] In one letter to his parents, Foote humorously described the Southern women whom he encountered by stating, "they are Generally—the female Sex—tall raw boned and long siff har uncomed and old home spun dresses ragged and dirty and generally go barefooted and very Coarse uncouth manners and generally no Education."[171] When his three year enlistment ended in 1865, the Union Army would not allow Foote to reenlist because of his age.[172] Although he pleaded to stay in the regiment, his age restricted him from further military service and he was honorably discharged shortly before the end of the war on February 22, 1865.[173] Foote later talked about his war experiences in an interview with Olive Deane Hormel. Together, Foote and Hormel used the interview to create his autobiography, titled *With Sherman to the Sea: a Drummer's Story of the Civil War*.

After the Civil War, Foote was a very active member of Genesee County. On November 3, 1874, he married Mary Holmes and the couple moved to Flint. They had two children, Kate and Hugh.[174] Foote was a businessman in Flint for many years. He managed a tin shop, and later took an interest in the roofing business.[175] However, Foote's contributions to Genesee County were not only limited to his financial pursuits. He was one of the first five hundred members of the Grand Army of the Republic's local Governor Crapo Post, and was an active member since its founding in 1884.[176] Perhaps one of the most interesting and meaningful

---

[170] *Portrait and Biographical Record of Genesee, Lapeer and Tuscola Counties, Michigan.*

[171] Corydon Edward Foote and Olive Deane Hormel, *With Sherman to the Sea; A Drummer Boy's Story of the Civil War, as Related by Corydon Edward Foote to Olive Deane Hormel* (Ann Arbor: University of Michigan, 1960), 130.

[172] "Corydon Foote, Flint's Last Veteran of the Civil War, Succumbs at 95," *The Flint Journal*, January 10, 1944.

[173] *Portrait and Biographical Record of Genesee, Lapeer and Tuscola Counties, Michigan.*

[174] *Portrait and Biographical Record of Genesee, Lapeer and Tuscola Counties, Michigan.*

[175] "Corydon Foote, Flint's Last Veteran of the Civil War, Succumbs at 95," *The Flint Journal*, January 10, 1944.

[176] "Corydon Foote, Flint's Last Veteran of the Civil War, Succumbs at 95," *The Flint*

impacts that he had in the Flint area came from his interest in birds. As an avid nature lover, Foote owned an assortment of stuffed birds and other animals that he displayed in his house for years. He eventually donated the collection to the Oak Grove Museum.[177] The collection still exists, and is located in the Foote Bird Museum at the For-Mar Nature Preserve and Arboretum.[178] Corydon Foote was Flint's last surviving veteran of the Civil War, and therefore was able to educate future generations with firsthand accounts about the war and the soldiers who were involved in it. Foote continued to serve as a living tribute to those who fought in the Civil War until he died of a heart attack on January 10, 1944, just one day after his ninety-fifth birthday.[179] He is buried at Evergreen Cemetery in Grand Blanc.

Foote Bird Museum, For-Mar Nature Preserve (author photo)

James W. Armstrong

While fighting they should remember that they were the representatives of the State of Michigan; and never must give up

---

Journal, January 10, 1944.
[177] "Corydon Foote, Flint's Last Veteran of the Civil War, Succumbs at 95," *The Flint Journal*, January 10, 1944.
[178] For-Mar Nature Preserve and Arboretum, "The Foote Bird Museum," http://www.geneseecountyparks.org/pages/formar (accessed February 9, 2012).
[179] "Corydon Foote, Flint's Last Veteran of the Civil War, Succumbs at 95," *The Flint Journal*, January 10, 1944.

that flag which the patriotic ladies of the City of Flint had so kindly presented to them, to be defended against the ravages of a Southern Guerilla band of Rebels and murderers.[180]

—James W. Armstrong, 10th Michigan Infantry

James W. Armstrong was born in Erie County, New York, in 1818.[181] According to land records, by 1836 he had moved to Clayton Twp., where he owned eighty acres.[182] He enlisted in the 10th Michigan Infantry in Flint on April 21, 1862. The following July, he was promoted to Commissary Sergeant of the regiment.[183] When not engaged in battle, the 10th Michigan was often involved in reconnaissance, protecting trains and building fortifications. While performing these duties, Armstrong and his comrades were frequently the victims of guerilla warfare. He detested them, saying:

> . . . But all that we have to guard against are guerilla bands of horsemen who rove through the country, making dashes at the cars, tearing up the track, burning water-tanks, and firing cotton. The latter we can see burning every night in some direction. The horsemen are what we might call our neighbors; for there are plantations in sight of our camp, whose owners are engaged in this type of warfare. We meet with them and they pretend to be Union men; but the fact is, we do not know who our friends are here: and more, I do not believe there is a man in this Valley whose sentiments are not with the South.[184]

Besides his regular criticism of these Southern guerillas, Armstrong also described a number of other interesting events during his service. For instance, he wrote about a slave named Susan Hall and her child, who

---

[180] James W. Armstrong, letter in *Wolverine Citizen*, May 16, 1863.
[181] Fletcher Willis Hewes, *History of the Formation, Movements, Camps, Scouts and Battles of the Tenth Regiment Michigan Volunteer Infantry* (Detroit: John Slater's Book and Job Printing Establishment, 1864), 159; Sons of Union Veterans, "Graves Registration: Department of Michigan," http://www.suvcwmi.org/graves/search.php (accessed May 18, 2012).
[182] Clayton Township is located between Flushing and Swartz Creek; Ellis, 355-356.
[183] Hewes, 159.
[184] James W. Armstrong, letter in *Wolverine Citizen*, September 13, 1862.

were being sent to Saginaw to live with the family of Captain Lyons. According to Armstrong, she was the slave of Isaac Winston, a plantation owner who had murdered Captain Lyons' servant. Susan's husband, Jacob, stole Winston's horse and rode to the Union camp. He told the 10th Michigan that Winston had indeed committed the murder, and took them to the body. The regiment then took possession of the plantation and seized the slaves. Winston, however, had fled before they arrived. Captain Lyons agreed to let Susan and her son live with his family in Saginaw. In return, Jacob stayed with the Union Army and was employed as the Captain's servant, with the agreement that the family would be reunited at war's end.[185] Armstrong wrote home frequently during the war, and his letters are full of interesting stories such as the one previously described. Most of these letters can be found in publications of the *Wolverine Citizen* from 1862 and 1863.

After the war, Armstrong returned to Flint, where he resided for a number of years with his wife Almira and their children. According to census records, the couple continued to live in Genesee County until at least 1870, where he worked as a millwright.[186] However, during the final years of his life, James and his wife moved to Ludington, Michigan. He died on July 9, 1896, and is buried in Lakeview Cemetery in Ludington.[187] Ironically, there is also a James W. Armstrong from the 5th Michigan Cavalry buried in Flushing Cemetery. Therefore, it is important to note that these are not the same people.

14th MICHIGAN INFANTRY

The 14th Michigan Infantry mustered into service on February 13, 1862, and was sent to join General Grant's army in the Western Theater. Later that year, the regiment fought at Corinth, Mississippi, and Lavergne, Tennessee.[188] In January 1863, it was engaged at the Battle of Stones

---

[185] James W. Armstrong, letter in *Wolverine Citizen*, September 13, 1862.
[186] Familysearch.org, "United States Census, 1850," https://familysearch.org/pal:/MM9.3.1/TH-266-11686-57991-8?cc=1438024 (accessed May 18, 2012).
[187] Sons of Union Veterans, "Graves Registration: Department of Michigan," http://www.suvcwmi.org/graves/search.php (accessed May 18, 2012).
[188] *Record of Service of Michigan Volunteers in the Civil War, 1861-1865, 14th Michigan Infantry*, 1.

River, and it remained on active duty in Tennessee for the remainder of the year. Meanwhile, after confiscating a large number of horses belonging to Southern sympathizers, the 14th Michigan became a regiment of mounted infantry. In 1864, over 400 soldiers reenlisted in the unit, assuming that it would continue to be a mounted regiment. However, despite Colonel Mizner's protests, an order was issued which forced the 14th Michigan to become a dismounted unit once again.[189] In June 1864, the regiment joined General Sherman's army, and actively participated in the Atlanta Campaign. During the campaign, the 14th Michigan fought honorably at Jonesboro, where it charged the Confederate line and captured four cannons, 300 men, and a general. After the surrender of Atlanta, the regiment took part in Sherman's "March to the Sea." Once Savannah, Georgia, was captured, the 14th Michigan participated in the invasion of the Carolinas. In March 1865, it was heavily engaged at Averysboro, North Carolina. Soon after, the regiment fought at Bentonville, North Carolina, where George Clute earned the Medal of Honor for capturing an enemy flag. The regiment served honorably until the end of the war, and mustered out of service on July 18, 1865.[190]

George W. Clute

Clute's grave (author photo)

---

[189]*Record of Service of Michigan Volunteers in the Civil War, 1861-1865, 14th Michigan Infantry*, 2.

[190]*Record of Service of Michigan Volunteers in the Civil War, 1861-1865, 14th Michigan Infantry*, 2-3.

George W. Clute, a long-time resident of Mount Morris, Michigan, was a Medal of Honor recipient. Clute was born on June 11, 1842, in Marathon Township of Lapeer County. At the age of nineteen, he dropped out of school. In 1862, while residing in Lapeer County, he enlisted in the 14th Michigan Infantry.[191] While serving in the Union Army, Clute fell in love with Loretta Owen of Mount Morris. According to his obituary in the *Flint Journal*, the couple was married on February 14, 1865.[192] During the final months of the war, Clute distinguished himself at the Battle of Bentonville, North Carolina, on March 19 for successfully capturing a Confederate flag. For his bravery, Clute was awarded the Congressional Medal of Honor. His citation read, "In a charge, captured the flag of the 20th North Carolina (C.S.A.), the flag being taken in a personal encounter with an officer who carried and defended it."[193] When describing the event, Clute later stated:

> In the midst of the struggle I saw a Confederate flag and made a rush for it. It was in the hands of their lieutenant. He and I were out of ammunition. Nothing but a trial of strength could determine which one of us was entitled to those colors. We had a desperate fight, but I proved to be the stronger and dragged the color-bearer and flag along for over 100 feet before he let go of the staff and ran back to his lines.[194]

A few minutes after the flag was taken, the same Confederate came across Clute in the midst of battle. In an act of vengeance, he shot Clute in the right arm with his revolver, and Clute never saw the man again.[195] Less than a month after the Battle of Bentonville, General Lee surrendered at Appomattox Court House.

---

[191] "George Clute, G. A. R. Dead at Morris," *Flint Journal*, February 18, 1919.
[192] "George Clute, G. A. R. Dead at Morris," *Flint Journal*, February 18, 1919.
[193] Congressional Medal of Honor Society, "Clute, George W.," *Congressional Medal of Honor Recipients*, http://www.cmohs.org/recipient-detail/266/clute-george-w.php (accessed February 9, 2012).
[194] W. F. Beyer and O. F. Keydel, *Deeds of Valor; How America's Civil War Heroes Won the Congressional Medal of Honor* (Detroit, MI: Perrien-Keydel Co., 1903. Republished in Stamford, CT: Longmeadow Press, 1994), 491.
[195] W. F. Beyer and O. F. Keydel, 492.

After the war, Clute returned to his wife in Genesee County. They lived in Thetford Township for nearly thirty years, but eventually moved to Mount Morris, where he spent the final twenty years of his life. As a citizen in the area, he became very active in local politics. He was the president of the village of Mount Morris for a number of years. During that time, he ordered the construction of the first cement sidewalk in Mount Morris, and later coordinated the development of over four miles of sidewalk in the community.[196] Clute was a member of the Fred W. Walker Post of the Grand Army of the Republic, and helped in the arrangements of the community's Memorial Day ceremonies on an annual basis. He died on February 13, 1919, and is buried in Mount Morris Cemetery.[197] A historical marker was erected at Bentonville honoring Clute's actions, and is viewable on the battlefield's driving tour.

Field at Bentonville where George Clute earned the Medal of Honor, referred to as "The Bull Pen" (author photo)

16th MICHIGAN INFANTRY

The 16th Michigan Infantry was mustered into service on September 8, 1861, and was originally commanded by Colonel Thomas Baylis Whitmarsh Stockton of Flint. The following summer, it took part in McClellan's Peninsula Campaign, and was engaged at Hanover Courthouse, Gaines' Mills, Malvern Hill, and Second Manassas. On

---

[196] "George Clute, G. A. R. Dead at Morris," *Flint Journal*, February 18, 1919.
[197] "George Clute, G. A. R. Dead at Morris," *Flint Journal*, February 18, 1919.

September 17, 1862, the regiment was present at Antietam, but was not engaged. Three months later, it took part in the assault at Fredericksburg, and suffered heavy casualties.[198] In May 1863, the 16th Michigan fought desperately at Chancellorsville. That summer, it was engaged at Gettysburg, and played a critical role in the defense of Little Round Top on July 2, 1863. In 1864, the regiment fought at the Wilderness, Spotsylvania, Cold Harbor, and Peebles' Farm. During the closing stages of the war, the 16th Michigan participated in the Petersburg Campaign, and aided in the capture of Richmond, Virginia. It mustered out of service on July 8, 1865.[199]

Thomas Baylis Whitmarsh Stockton

The saddest day in my life —Some 50,000 men, *Freemen*, they are called, were drawn up in columns today and bid a sad farewell to their chosen, and honored commander. Tell for those in power that Gen'l. McClellan is an honest and true patriot for had he but said the word and I truly believe the whole of them, yes, the whole army of the Potomac, would have thrown down their arms, or at least follow him back to Washington and demand his restoration. Washington never had truer followers than McClellan.[200]

—T. B. W. Stockton, 16th Michigan Infantry

During the first years of the Civil War, the 16th Michigan Infantry was commanded by Colonel T. B. W. Stockton of Flint, Michigan. Stockton was born on June 18, 1805, in Walton, New York. At age seventeen he applied to the United States Military Academy at West Point, where he became skilled as a soldier and an engineer.[201] Following his graduation from West Point, Stockton was stationed at various forts along

---

[198] *Record of Service of Michigan Volunteers in the Civil War, 1861-1865, 16th Michigan Infantry*, 1-2.
[199] *Record of Service of Michigan Volunteers in the Civil War, 1861-1865, 16th Michigan Infantry*, 1-3.
[200] Colonel Stockton's Civil War Diary, November 10, 1862, Genesee Historical Collections Center at the University of Michigan-Flint, Flint, MI.
[201] Dennis McMullen, *Colonel T. B. W. Stockton: Soldier, Engineer, Businessman* (Flint: University of Michigan-Flint Archives, 1988), 1.

the frontier, and was at one point even commanded by future president Zachary Taylor.[202] Stockton remained on the frontier from 1828 to 1831, where he was involved in exploring new territories and classifying various Indian tribes. During this time, he met Maria G. Smith, daughter of Jacob Smith,[203] and they were married on March 3, 1830. This marriage proved crucial to Stockton's later involvement in Genesee County, simply because the land that he owned in Flint came as a result of his prosperous wife's inheritance.[204] During the Mexican-American War, he became Colonel of the First Michigan Volunteers. The regiment was sent to Mexico but was not engaged in fighting. In 1852, Stockton and his family moved to California in search of gold, and resided there until his return to Flint in 1858.[205]

Even before the Civil War, Stockton greatly contributed to the development of not only Genesee County, but to the advancement of the entire Michigan Territory. Because of his skills in topographical engineering, he helped in the construction of bridges and roads throughout the Lower Peninsula. Furthermore, Stockton helped improve the condition of harbors along the Great Lakes.[206] He helped in the foundation of the Genesee County Agricultural Society and many of the county fairs were held on his property.[207] His skills as a military leader proved beneficial to the county as well, and he served as captain of the local militia, referred to as the "Flint Union Greys."[208]

Upon the outbreak of the Civil War, Stockton was eager to join the struggle to lay down the Rebellion. In September 1861 he organized the 16th Michigan Infantry in response to Lincoln's call for more troops. Because of his crucial role in founding the 16th Michigan, the unit was commonly referred to as "Stockton's Independent Regiment." There were men from Genesee County in nine of the regiment's companies. In fact, one was even given the nickname "The Genesee Company" because of its high percentage of men from the Flint area.[209] Under Stockton's

---

[202] McMullen, 2.
[203] Maria Smith was the daughter of Jacob Smith, the first white settler in the Flint area.
[204] McMullen, 2-3.
[205] McMullen, 12-13.
[206] McMullen, 3-8.
[207] The Stockton Center at Spring Grove, "Thomas and Maria Stockton," http://stocktoncenter.org/Thomas&Maria/index.html (accessed January 22, 2012).
[208] McMullen, 13.
[209] Ellis, 86.

command, the 16th Michigan partook in numerous battles, notably the engagement at Gaines Mill on June 27, 1862. The conflict proved to be disastrous for the regiment, which suffered nearly seventy-five percent casualties.[210] Stockton himself, along with many of his men, was captured by the Confederates and sent to Libby Prison near Richmond, Virginia.[211] During his time as a prisoner, he was visited by General Robert E. Lee, a long-time friend from West Point. Stockton also met with his nephew, Confederate General James Longstreet. Meanwhile, another Confederate nephew, George Deas, refused to visit Stockton because of his ties with the Union.[212] Nonetheless, because of their familial connection, Longstreet made Stockton's imprisonment as comfortable as possible, and Stockton was released after only two months.[213] In September 1862, he returned to the Union Army and was placed in command of the entire brigade. As commander of the Third Brigade, First Division, Fifth Corps, Stockton commanded the 16th Michigan, 20th Maine, "Brady's Company" of Michigan Sharpshooters, 12th New York, 17th New York, 44th New York, 83rd Pennsylvania and 1st U. S. Sharpshooters.[214] He led the brigade at Antietam, and vividly described the gruesome results of the battle by writing, "The graves were many, the trees were cut off by shot from our batteries. Found one poor female weeping over the grave where some of her relatives had been buried. How many other desolate ones this battle has made."[215] He participated in the battles at Fredericksburg and Chancellorsville and eventually resigned from the military on May 18, 1863, at the age of 57.[216] Less than two months after his resignation the 16th Michigan, 44th New York, 83rd Pennsylvania and 20th Maine became legendary for their stubborn defense of Little Round Top during the Battle of Gettysburg.

After the Civil War, Stockton continued to shape Genesee County. He and his wife Maria donated twenty acres of land to the Michigan

---

[210] A "casualty" refers to any soldier who is absent from the line of duty. They do not necessarily have to be dead, but are also considered casualties if they are wounded, captured or missing.
[211] McMullen, 21.
[212] Gregory M. Havrilcsak, "Thomas Baylis Whitmarsh Stockton: A Brief Talk" (A speech presented during the dedication of the Michigan Historical Marker for the Stockton Home, 2005), 6. Unpublished manuscript in possession of author.
[213] The Stockton Center at Spring Grove. "Thomas and Maria Stockton".
[214] McMullen, 22.
[215] Colonel Stockton's Civil War Diary, September 26, 1862.
[216] McMullen, 23.

School for the Deaf, Dumb and Blind. Furthermore, Stockton's wife founded the Ladies' Library Association, which later became the foundation for Flint's first public library.[217] The Stockton family was extremely active in real estate development, and owned property extending from the Flint River, south to Court Street and east to Church Street. This section of land became part of Flint's early business district, and had a crucial impact on the city's expansion and economic growth.[218] Stockton died on December 13, 1890, at age eighty-five. He is buried at Glenwood Cemetery in Flint, Michigan.[219] His house was restored and turned into a museum, and is located on Ann Arbor Street in Flint. His nephew, George Deas, served as a Lieutenant in the Confederate Army, and is also buried at Glenwood.

Although Stockton was indeed very beneficial to both the community and the nation, he was not without flaws. Shortly after marrying his wife in 1830, Stockton was assigned to a military post in Detroit. During that time, he owned two slaves: Rachel and her son James Henry.[220] Eventually he sold Rachel and James to William Walker in St. Louis, Missouri. Rachel then sued Walker for their freedom. She claimed that because she and her son lived in Michigan, which was a free territory at the time, they were no longer slaves but free persons. Therefore, Walker had no right to buy them. Initially, the St. Louis Circuit Court ruled against Rachel, saying that because Stockton was in the military he was not able to choose where the government stationed him to live. However, Rachel appealed to the Missouri Supreme Court in 1836. In the case *Rachel v. Walker*, the Court decided that if a military officer took his slave into a free territory, he lost the ownership rights to that slave. Rachel was given her freedom.[221] This court case certainly brought out a side of Stockton that most people do not want to hear about. It is an unpleasant story that most historians and organizations in Flint avoid shedding light upon. Instead, they only emphasize Stockton's achievements, while turning a blind eye when examining his downfalls. Nevertheless, history

---

[217] The Stockton Center at Spring Grove, "Thomas and Maria Stockton".
[218] McMullen, 27.
[219] McMullen, 38.
[220] Missouri State Archives, "Rachel v. William Walker (1836)," *Before Dred Scott: Freedom Suits in Antebellum Missouri*, http://www.sos.mo.gov/archives/education/aahi/beforedredscott/rachelV.asp (accessed January 22, 2012).
[221] Missouri State Archives.

must be told in its entirety, both the good and the bad. Stockton's ownership of slaves has permanently scarred his reputation according to the standards of modern society. However, it is important to remember that while he was flawed, just like any other human being is, he nonetheless had many accomplishments in Flint and in other parts of the nation. By measuring his accomplishments against his downfalls, it is apparent that Stockton was a more complex individual than historians have previously described.

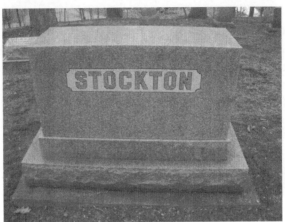

The grave of Colonel Stockton (author photo)

Ziba B. Graham

Old tobacco chewers who have never before known the want of the *weed*, now go around as if they had lost their best friend; really they command pity. They look so mutely, and yet so eloquently into each others faces, the no one can misunderstand them. "Stranger, haven't you got an extra chaw," is written as plainly upon their phiz, and as readily understood as if spoken; the old tobacco codger who can tell where his next quid is to come from, is considered a lucky fellow.[222]

—Ziba B. Graham, 16th Michigan Infantry

---

[222] Ziba B. Graham, letter in *Wolverine Citizen*, September 13, 1862.

Because he only fought during the first half of the Civil War, Stockton's diary lacked a sense of conclusiveness and tends to leave readers wondering about the fate of the 16th Michigan during the remainder of the war. Fortunately, Genesee County resident Ziba B. Graham's recollections picked up right where Stockton's had ended. Graham was born on April 19, 1839, in Calais, Maine, and lived there until his father James W. Graham relocated the family to Flushing, Michigan, in 1856. [223] Originally, he had planned on pursuing a career in business, but became eager to fight for the preservation of the Union at the outbreak of the Civil War in 1861. At only twenty-two years of age, Graham became one of the first citizens from Genesee County to enter the struggle against the rebellion. He enlisted in Flint on August 1, 1861, joining as a sergeant in Company C of the 16th Michigan Infantry. Graham agreed to a three-year enlistment in the regiment. A year after joining the unit, he was promoted to Second Lieutenant on August 30, 1862. In March 1863, he transferred to Company G and was commissioned to First Lieutenant of Company I on April 22, 1863.[224]

As a member of the 16th Michigan, Graham was accustomed to a life of combat. His regiment was a part of many prominent battles, including engagements at Second Manassas and Gaines' Mill. He also experienced the horrors of Fredericksburg as the 16th Michigan assaulted Confederates on Marye's Heights. While speaking at a Grand Army of the Republic[225] reunion in 1892, Graham recalled the events that unfolded at Fredericksburg. During his speech, he made special mention of his comrade George D. Sidman, an Owosso resident who had won the Medal of Honor at Gaines' Mill and who had shown the same bravery at Fredericksburg. Graham recalled Sidman's role in the battle by saying:

> Well do I remember that day in 1862, as we stood *en masse* on Stafford Heights, overlooking Fredericksburg, all ready to cross the Rappahannock, when the first brigade colors for our brigade were brought upon the field. I can see now the eagerness with which this comrade Sidman, a mere boy, with scarce the down of young manhood upon his chin, sprang forward from the ranks and begged of me the permission to carry those colors. It was granted.

---

[223] "Death of Capt. Z. B. Graham," *Flushing Observer*, August 15, 1901.
[224] "Death of Capt. Z. B. Graham," *Flushing Observer*, August 15, 1901.
[225] The Grand Army of the Republic (G.A.R.) was an organization of Union veterans who served in the Civil War.

Colonel Stockton in command, admiring his pluck but depreciating his youth, finally gave his consent. Sidman brought them out of that hell of fire, many holes shot in them, himself wounded. On his breast to-day he wears the Medal of Honor, a patent of nobility for bravery far above riches and above price.[226]

For Graham, the horrors of battle did not end at Fredericksburg. He and the 16th Michigan were heavily engaged during the second day of Gettysburg on July 2, 1863. While Joshua Chamberlain and the 20th Maine became legendary for valiantly defending the southeastern side of Little Round Top, the 16th Michigan's role in defending the southwestern portion of the hill was just as crucial. Though the regiment successfully fought off Confederate attacks, its victory did not come without sacrifice. Graham lost almost half of the men in his company alone, and the regiment as a whole suffered nearly sixty casualties.[227]

Surprisingly, Graham did not demonstrate feelings of vengeance towards the Rebels after losing so many of his comrades. In fact, after Pickett's Charge on July 3, he was very merciful towards his opponents. In his diary, he recalled encountering a number of Confederate wounded who were begging for water. Upon seeing that the well crank had been removed, he learned from a Rebel that the owner of the house had taken it in order to prevent the Confederates from getting water. He found the man hiding in his cellar, who steadfastly refused to give him the crank. After threatening to shoot the man, Graham was finally given the crank and gave water to the wounded.[228]

Almost a year after the fighting at Gettysburg, Graham was severely wounded on May 23, 1864, at the Battle of North Anna. After reaching the rank of Captain, he was mustered out of service on September 7, 1864 (less than four months after receiving his wound).[229] After the war, Graham returned to Genesee County. He married a Flushing resident named Retta Kent, who was the daughter of a local reverend.

---

[226] J. W. Jones, *The Story of American Heroism: Thrilling Narratives of Personal Adventures during the Great Civil War* (Akron, Ohio: The Werner Company, 1896), 129.
[227] Ziba Graham, *On To Gettysburg. Ten Days from My Diary of 1863* (Detroit: Winn & Hammond, Printers, 1893), 11.
[228] Ziba Graham, *On To Gettysburg. Ten Days from My Diary of 1863*, 13.
[229] "Death of Capt. Z. B. Graham," *Flushing Observer*, August 15, 1901.

They later had two children, a son and a daughter.[230] In the years following the Civil War, Graham and his wife moved to Saginaw, where he worked in the lumber industry. The couple moved several times, and lived in Saginaw, Flint, and Bay City. However, they eventually settled down in Detroit, where they resided for more than twenty years of their married life.[231] In May 1901, Graham was diagnosed with sclerosis of the liver. He returned to the city of Flushing and resided in his brother's house on Elm Street. Ziba B. Graham died on the morning of Tuesday, August 13, 1901, at around seven o'clock.[232] He is buried in the Flushing Cemetery.

Although Graham did not have the financial resources that Stockton had, he was able to contribute to the culture of Genesee County in a different way. Whereas Stockton helped develop the physical aspects of Flint and its surrounding area, Graham gave its citizens a sense of honor by recalling the heroic deeds of local soldiers. While in the service, Graham frequently corresponded with Genesee County newspapers. Through a series of letters written to *The Wolverine Citizen* and to other local newspapers, he discussed the 16th Michigan's movements and engagements. Moreover, he used his letters to describe the bravery of his fallen comrades. Graham's testimonials proved comforting to many local families, as he gave accounts of the heroic last moments of their deceased relatives.[233] For instance, on July 12, 1862, *The Wolverine Citizen* printed a letter that Graham wrote to Mrs. T. C. Carr[234] in consolation for her husband's recent death. A portion of the letter read:

> He was struck down by a grape-shot—Poor Captain! he was the first man in our Regiment whose life was called for as an offering for his country's salvation. He was within a foot of me when he fell: he died without a groan. I can add nothing to alleviate the sorrow of thy heart. I can only add that our Captain's death was most fearfully avenged."[235]

---

[230] "Death of Capt. Z. B. Graham," *Flushing Observer*, August 15, 1901.
[231] "Death of Capt. Z. B. Graham," *Flushing Observer*, August 15, 1901.
[232] "Death of Capt. Z. B. Graham," *Flushing Observer*, August 15, 1901.
[233] "Death of Capt. Z. B. Graham," *Flushing Observer*, August 15, 1901.
[234] Full name not known.
[235] Ziba B. Graham, "Letter to Mrs. T. C. Carr," *Wolverine Citizen*, July 12, 1862.

Likewise, Graham made Genesee County residents feel more connected to the war. He did not only write about battles and suffering, but gave his readers an opportunity to experience the daily life of a Civil War soldier as well. While Graham's writings tended to be very serious and blunt, some of the comments that he made were quite humorous. Perhaps most comical was a passage that he wrote after having dental work done, which read:

> All being quiet in our front, I received permission to go back to the hospital to get an ugly tooth extracted that had kept me dancing all the night before. Our surgeon, Doctor [Robert] Everett, who had been hard at work all night at the amputation table, made but short work and little ado about one tooth. He laid me on the ground, straddled me, and with a formidable pair of nippers pulled and yanked me around until either the tooth had to come out, or my head off. I was glad when the head conquered. I then made up my mind never to go to a surgeon for a tooth-pulling matinee the day after a fight.[236]

Obviously, many other soldiers from the Flint area experienced the same hardships and situations that Graham faced during the war. However, Graham stood out among these soldiers because he was one of the few men from the area to actually take the time to get his words published and make them accessible to the community. As a veteran, Graham became very involved in the Grand Army of the Republic and attended annual reunions with the survivors of the 16th Michigan.[237] In Detroit on March 2, 1889, he read a portion of his diary to the Military Order of the Loyal Legion of the United States. This section of his diary was later published under the title *On To Gettysburg. Ten Days from My Diary of 1863*.[238] Because his diary was published and is now accessible to the entire nation, Graham's experiences provided Genesee County with a voice with which to tell its role in the Civil War. Therefore, his writings gave the Flint area a sense of self-identity.

---

[236] Graham, *On To Gettysburg. Ten Days from My Diary of 1863*.
[237] "Death of Capt. Z. B. Graham," *Flushing Observer*, August 15, 1901.
[238] Graham, *On To Gettysburg. Ten Days from My Diary of 1863*.

The grave of Ziba Graham (author photo)

Randolph W. Ransom

Captain Randolph W. Ransom, of your city, has fallen another victim to the cause of Liberty. A more gallant, a better beloved officer, could not be found. Respected as a gentleman and as a brave officer, he had entwined himself around the hearts of his company, and his fellow officers, all of whom keenly feel the loss.[239]

—Ziba B. Graham, 16th Michigan Infantry

Stockton and Graham were only two of many brave Genesee County soldiers in the 16th Michigan. For instance, Randolph W. Ransom, a Flint resident, eagerly answered Lincoln's call to preserve the Union. After the Federals were soundly defeated at the First Battle of Bull Run, Ransom enlisted in Company C, better known as the "Genesee Light Guard." Although he initially served as a 2nd Lieutenant, he was quickly promoted to 1st Lieutenant less than two weeks after his enlistment.[240]

After illustrating exemplary bravery and good conduct at Hanover Court House, Ransom was promoted to Captain, a position which had previously been held by the deceased Thomas C. Carr. However, during

---

[239] Ziba B. Graham, letter in *Wolverine Citizen*, September 13, 1862.
[240] Ellis, 92.

the time of his promotion, Ransom was suffering from illness and fever, and was in a hospital near Portsmouth. This sickness prevented him from being engaged during the Seven Days Battles of June 25 to July 1, 1862. However, Ransom's distaste of hospitals caused him to return to the ranks prematurely. As Ziba Graham so eloquently put it, "He, like every true soldier, viewed a hospital with more horror than a bayonet charge—left it before he was able for duty, and rejoined his Regiment at Harrison Landing."[241] For a time, he was too weak to march, and followed the regiment on horseback. However, by the time the Second Battle of Bull Run was underway, Ransom's health was improving. Nonetheless, he was still weak from the illness, and many of his comrades pleaded with him to return to the rear rather than participate in the battle. Ransom refused, remembering that his "Genesee Boys" looked to him for leadership. The regiment was heavily engaged at the Second Battle of Bull Run and sustained heavy casualties. By nightfall on August 30, 1862, seventy-nine men were killed or wounded, and seventeen more were missing. Unfortunately, Ransom was one of the deceased.[242] When describing his comrade's death, Graham recollected:

> . . . and with this indomitable will, this determination not to give way to the weakness with which his late sickness had left him, he brought his little band of followers into the field, and with his sword raised toward heaven, and with a loud voice, which arose above the din of battle, he bid his boys stand true, assuring us that we could whip the rebels. At this instant he fell, pierced through the brain by a bullet. Thus another brave has fallen. Again are the "Genesee Boys" without a Captain.[243]

The citizens of Genesee County did not forget Ransom's sacrifice. The Flushing G.A.R. Post 89 was named the "Ransom Post" in his honor.[244] In the years following the Civil War, his family continued to play a significant role in the community. In fact, his nephew Albert later became the editor for the *Flushing Observer*.[245] Another nephew, Ransler B.

---

[241] Ziba B. Graham, letter in *Wolverine Citizen*, September 13, 1862.
[242] Ellis, 89.
[243] Ziba B. Graham, letter in *Wolverine Citizen*, September 13, 1862.
[244] James T. Lyons, "Post Charters on File," *Sons of Union Veterans*, http://www.suvcwmi.org/gar/charters.pdf (accessed April 20, 2012).

Ransom, was a member of the 4th Michigan Cavalry and aided in the capture of Jefferson Davis.[246] Randolph W. Ransom is buried in Flushing Cemetery, near Coutant Street. His descendants still reside in Genesee County even to this day.

Thomas C. Carr

As previously mentioned, Ziba B. Graham wrote in-detail about the death of another Genesee County resident, Thomas C. Carr. In the opening stages of the war, Carr headed a recruiting station in Flint. During this time, he played an active role in enlisting men into the Genesee Light Guard.[247] After raising the regiment in the summer of 1861, Carr led the men to Camp Backus in Detroit, where they met with the rest of the regiment. For the next several months, Carr served as Captain of the company, while Randolph W. Ransom served directly under him as a Lieutenant.[248]

On June 27, 1862, the 16th Michigan found itself engaged in a desperate struggle at Gaines' Mill, Virginia. Carr was the first man in the regiment to be killed during the battle. The day proved disastrous for the regiment: forty-nine men were killed, one hundred and sixteen were wounded and an additional fifty-five were missing. Colonel Stockton himself was captured during the battle, and was later sent to Libby Prison. Carr is buried in Metamora Cemetery.[249]

Isaac Wixom

Isaac Wixom was a renowned surgeon in the 16th Michigan. He was born March 7, 1803, in Hector, New York. Early in his life, Wixom took an interest in the study of medicine, and he graduated from the

---

[245] Wood, 702.
[246] Ellis, 107.
[247] The Genesee Light Guard was the name given to Company C of the 16th Michigan Infantry. Many of its men had previously come from another group, referred to as the "Flushing Light Artillery."
[248] Ellis, 86.
[249] Don and Lois Harvey, "Michigan Veterans of the Civil War: Burial Sites," *Michigan in the War*, http://www.michiganinthewar.org/c.htm (accessed April 20, 2012).

Medical Society of Pen Yan in Yates County, New York. Soon after, he married Maria Ryal. In 1829, Wixom and his wife moved to Farmington, Michigan, where he practiced medicine. In 1845 he moved to Argentine in Genesee County, and worked in the milling and mercantile business. However, he found life as a doctor more suitable, and once again opened his practice.[250] In 1838, he was elected as a representative in the state legislature. During his term, he was on the House Committee for Education, and helped in founding the University of Michigan. He was later elected to the state Senate in 1841, where he helped draw up one of Michigan's first railroad charters.[251] After retiring from politics, he continued working as a physician. In 1845, Wixom performed the first successful amputation of the hip-joint in the United States. He also taught medical and surgical skills to nearly forty students, most of whom later became doctors themselves.[252]

When the Civil War began in 1861, Wixom helped Colonel Stockton enlist recruits in Flint and its neighboring communities. He was appointed as the surgeon of the 16th Michigan, and followed the regiment into twenty-two battles. In 1863, he resigned from the position due to poor health. In 1869, he moved from Argentine to Fenton.[253] Less than a year after his wife's death, Isaac Wixom passed away on July 24, 1880. He is buried in Oakwood Cemetery in Fenton. His granddaughter Emma Wixom, better known as Emma Nevada, became a popular opera singer in both the United States and Europe.[254]

21st MICHIGAN INFANTRY

After mustering into service on September 4, 1862, the 21st Michigan Infantry was immediately sent to fight in Kentucky, and was heavily engaged at the Battle of Perryville.[255] A short time later, the

---

[250] Eugene Gray, "Isaac Wixom Biography," *Michigan State University*, https://www.msu.edu/~graye/emma/IWixomBio.html (accessed April 23, 2012).
[251] Wood, 570.
[252] Eugene Gray, "Isaac Wixom Biography," *Michigan State University*.
[253] Wood, 570.
[254] Eugene Gray, "Emma Nevada," *Michigan State University*, https://www.msu.edu/~graye/emma/chronolo.html (accessed April 23, 2012).

regiment marched into Tennessee, where it fought at Lavergne and Stones River.[256] In 1863, it was engaged in a number of battles and skirmishes, but fought most desperately at Chickamauga. That October, the regiment assisted in the capture of Chattanooga, Tennessee. The following year, the 21st Michigan played an active role in Sherman's "March to the Sea." In 1865, the regiment participated in the invasion of the Carolinas, and met its last major engagement at Bentonville, North Carolina. While in Durham, North Carolina, it was present for the surrender of Confederate forces under Joseph Johnston. The 21st Michigan mustered out of service on June 8, 1865.[257]

William B. McCreery

The silver steel grows cloudy and lurid, the knives are busy, the saws play—it is bloody work. I see pale faces, bloody garments. True right arms that had offended by reason of their loyalty to the old flag are lopped like slips of golden willow. Feet that never turned from the foe, for ever more without an owner, strew the ground. I do not hear a moan—the very silence oppresses me—no sound save the gnawing of those terrible saws. It seems as if an accent of pain from some weary sufferer would be a welcome sound, and I think of a brave bird, wounded unto death, that I have held in my hand, its keen eye undimmed and full upon me, throbbing with the pain and the dying, and yet so silent.[258]

—William B. McCreery, 21st Michigan Infantry

The Fentons were closely linked to another prominent name in the Flint community: the McCreery family. This connection was formed when Colonel Fenton's daughter, Ada, married William Barker McCreery.

---

[255] The Battle of Perryville was the largest Civil War battle fought in Kentucky.
[256] *Record of Service of Michigan Volunteers in the Civil War, 1861-1865, 21st Michigan Infantry*, 1.
[257] *Record of Service of Michigan Volunteers in the Civil War, 1861-1865, 21st Michigan Infantry*, 2.
[258] William B. McCreery, *My Experience as a Prisoner of War, and Escape from Libby Prison* (Detroit: Winn & Hammond, 1893), 6.

McCreery was born in Mount Morris, New York, on August 27, 1836. His parents, Reuben McCreery and Susan Barker, moved to Flint when he was only three years old, and he spent the rest of his life residing there. When Governor Blair asked for recruits to lay down the Rebellion, McCreery joined Company F of the 2nd Michigan Infantry. The company was mainly comprised of the local militia, and referred to as "The Flint Union Greys."[259] He was later promoted to lieutenant colonel, and was placed in command of the 21st Michigan.[260]

McCreery faced a great deal of hardship during the war. He was seriously wounded at Williamsburg, Virginia, on May 5, 1862.[261] A year later, a rumor came to Flint about McCreery's death at the Battle of Chattanooga. After hearing the news, a friend of the family was sent to recover his body, carrying a message from the Adjutant General that read:

> The Bearer of this George S. Hopkins a loyal and highly respectable citizen of this State has been sent by the Father of Colonel McCreery reported killed in the late battle at Chattenoogo (*sic*) for the purpose of recovering his body and bringing it to this State. Officers in authority are most respectfully requested to afford him every facility in their power to enable him to accomplish his purpose.[262]

Contrary to his father's beliefs, William McCreery was very much alive. However, around the same time that Hopkins was sent to recover his body, McCreery was again wounded and captured at the Battle of Chickamauga.[263] Shortly after his capture, he was sent to Libby Prison in Richmond, Virginia. During his time there, he experienced the true deprivations of prison life. Upon arrival, he was searched by the Confederates, and anything of value was taken by them. Furthermore, McCreery learned that each prisoner was allowed to write two letters per

---

[259] Ellis, 63.
[260] "Colonel William B. McCreery Dead," *Wolverine Citizen*, December 12, 1896.
[261] "Colonel McCreery Answers the Last Roll Call," *Genesee Democrat*, December 12, 1896.
[262] *McCreery-Fenton Family Papers* (Ann Arbor: Bentley Historical Library, University of Michigan).
[263] "Colonel McCreery Answers the Last Roll Call," *Genesee Democrat*, December 12, 1896.

week. Each letter was required to be no more than six lines long, and was always read by prison authorities before being sent. If the letter mentioned anything about the harsh treatment of Union prisoners, it was immediately thrown away.[264] Conditions in the prison were horrific. The windows were nothing more than holes in the wall, there was a shortage of food, and insects constantly swarmed the prisoners. To combat boredom, the soldiers played cards and board games, organized a band of musicians, and took part in plays or educational lectures.[265]

Undoubtedly, McCreery and two of his fellow prisoners, Captain Skelton of Iowa and Lieutenant Williams of Indiana, were determined to regain their liberty. They bribed one of the guards, who said that he would allow them to escape if they each paid him twenty dollars. Luckily, McCreery had sewn three hundred dollars into the waistband of his pants, and the money had never been confiscated by the Confederates. Nonetheless, he felt physically unable to make the journey, but gave Skelton and Williams enough money to bribe the guard. Both men successfully escaped.[266] A short time later, McCreery also found a chance to regain his freedom. He learned that a group of inmates were in the process of digging a tunnel, and quickly joined in their efforts. On February 14, 1864, McCreery and 108 other prisoners attempted to escape. Fifty-eight were recaptured, but the other fifty-one made it safely back to Union lines.[267] Fortunately, McCreery was successful in his escape.

As a result of his wounds and the toll that Libby Prison had taken on his body, McCreery resigned from the military that September.[268] After returning home, he became a very prominent citizen in both Genesee County and the rest of the state. In the years following the Civil War, he wrote a detailed account of his escape, which was published under the title *My Experience as a Prisoner of War, and Escape from Libby Prison*. He was the mayor of Flint for two terms, and held the position of State Treasurer from 1875 to 1879. Under the Grant administration, he was the Collector of Internal Revenue.[269] McCreery served as President of the 21st

---

[264] McCreery, 8.
[265] McCreery, 16.
[266] McCreery, 15.
[267] McCreery, 18.
[268] "Colonel McCreery Answers the Last Roll Call," *Genesee Democrat*, December 12, 1896.
[269] "Colonel William B. McCreery Dead," *Wolverine Citizen*, December 12, 1896.

Michigan Infantry Association, and was an active member of the Crapo Post G. A. R. He was also the President of the Flint Water Works Company, as well as the acting Cashier of Flint's Citizens' National Bank. As if that was not enough, he spent eight years as a member on the State Board of Agriculture,[270] and served as United States Consul to Chile under the Harrison administration.[271] After reviewing this evidence, there is no doubt that McCreery was one of the most influential men in the history of Flint and its surrounding communities.

McCreery wanted his family's impact on the Flint community to be remembered. In 1885, he ordered the construction of the Fenton-McCreery monument in Glenwood Cemetery. Soon after its completion, *The Wolverine Citizen* praised the monument through a passage that read:

> It is worth a special visit to beautiful Glen-Wood, to view the Monument recently erected by Col. W. B. McCreery, as a memorial of the Fenton family and his own. Dotted as the grounds are with elegant family testimonials of love cherished by survivors for their dead, this one stands conspicuous in size, material, and artistic design. It is evidently very costly, but we do not care to make cost a factor in affectionate and reverential remembrances of the dear ones we have lost.[272]

In October 1896, McCreery suffered from a stroke that paralyzed him. He died only two months later on December 9, 1896, leaving behind a wife and three children.[273] Most of the McCreery family was buried next to the Fenton family plot, and the Fenton-McCreery monument in Glenwood Cemetery can still be visited today.

---

[270] "Colonel William B. McCreery Dead," *Wolverine Citizen*, December 12, 1896.
[271] "Colonel McCreery Answers the Last Roll Call," *Genesee Democrat*, December 12, 1896.
[272] "Glen-Wood Cemetery, The Fenton-McCreery Monument," *Wolverine Citizen*, October 10, 1885.
[273] "Colonel William B. McCreery Dead," *Wolverine Citizen*, December 12, 1896.

The Fenton-McCreery monument, Glenwood Cemetery (author photo)

23rd MICHIGAN INFANTRY

The 23rd Michigan Infantry mustered into service on September 13, 1862, and was assigned to the Western Theater. The regiment was given its first taste of battle at Paris, Kentucky on July 29, 1863. From that point onward, it was involved in campaigns throughout Kentucky and Tennessee, and participated in the defense of Knoxville, Tennessee, in September 1863. The following year, the regiment aided in the capture of Atlanta, and fought against forces under Confederate General John Bell Hood at the Battle of Franklin, Tennessee, in November 1864. In 1865, it fought in the Carolinas, and was instrumental in the capture Fort Anderson, located in North Carolina. The regiment mustered out of service on June 28, 1865.[274]

Rev. James S. Smart

I went around to some of the tents myself, to rally them, calling upon every man to turn out who could march a mile and shoot a

---

[274] *Record of Service of Michigan Volunteers in the Civil War, 1861-1865, 23rd Michigan Infantry*, 1-3.

rebel. Every man that could stand was soon on his feet, examining his gun and ammunition, ready for the fray. As the men straightened up and their eyes flashed, the universal exclamation was, "I can't march far, *but I can shoot.*" But the enemy did not appear.[275]

—James Smart, Chaplain of the 23rd Michigan Infantry

James Shirley Smart was born on March 31, 1825, in Searsport, Maine. He was the son of Ephraim Knight Smart, who was a local preacher, and Mary Hoyt Cass Smart. When James was only six years old, his father's sudden death robbed him of his childhood, and by age seven he was forced to leave home in order to find work. He was engaged in life at sea for a few years, but eventually returned to school and pursued an education. At age twenty-one, he moved to Michigan, and soon followed in his father's footsteps by taking up a life of preaching.[276] In 1851, while in St. Clair, he married Elmira Carter, and they later had eight children.[277] By the outbreak of the Civil War, he was the pastor of the Methodist Episcopal Church in Flint.

Smart was a zealous pastor, and was very outspoken about his moral convictions. He strongly opposed the consumption of alcohol, and abstained from it completely.[278] He was an ardent supporter of the Union, and openly criticized President Buchanan for not addressing the issue of secession. After Buchanan called for a nationwide day of fasting, Smart retorted, "James Buchanan proclaims a fast. It is well. Having brought the country to the brink of ruin, his administration appropriately goes out with humiliation, fasting and prayer."[279] Smart was also a fiery abolitionist, and the immorality of slavery was a frequent topic in his sermons. On January

---

[275] James Smart, letter in *Wolverine Citizen*, November 8, 1862.
[276] *Journal and Reports of the Thirty-Seventh Annual Session of the Detroit Conference of the Methodist Episcopal Church* (Detroit: Wm. Graham Printing Co., 1892), 56-57.
[277] Familysearch.org, "Michigan, County Marriages, 1820-1935," https://familysearch.org/pal:/MM9.3.1/TH-1-16784-65313-31?cc=1810350 (accessed June 18, 2012).
[278] *Journal and Reports of the Thirty-Seventh Annual Session of the Detroit Conference of the Methodist Episcopal Church*, 59.
[279] James Smart, *National Fast: A Fast Day Sermon* (Flint: William Stevenson, Publisher, 1861), 5.

4, 1861, Smart gave a speech in Flint, and showed his detestation for the institution altogether. He said:

> But the great crime of this nation is against another race. They were not found here, neither did the come here voluntarily. They were stolen from their homes in a far off land. Our mother country and our own conspired together to kindle the most horrid wars among the different tribes of Africa, by offering their gold or worthless trinkets for the prisoners that might be taken in those wars. Or, perhaps more often the slave traders, with their own hands, seized the poor Africans upon their native coasts, as a wolf would seize his prey, and dragged them despairing from their homes forever.[280]

By the summer of 1862, Smart felt inclined to join the war effort. He raised a company of 110 men, many of whom were members of his congregation, and enlisted in the 23rd Michigan Infantry. He became Captain of the company, which was known as the "Wolverine Guard," but later gave up the promotion to become Chaplain of the regiment.[281] While in the military, Smart frequently wrote home, and many of his letters were published in the *Wolverine Citizen*. Notably, he praised the women of Genesee County for their donations and dedication to the war effort, stating, "Many a heart became larger, and many a brave eye was filled with grateful tears, as the exclamation was uttered, 'God bless my wife!' 'God bless that mother!' 'God bless this dear sister!' 'God bless the ladies of old Genesee!' And to it all, I most heartily say, Amen."[282] Smart served as Chaplain of the regiment for nearly a year, but he ultimately resigned his position and was honorably discharged on July 31, 1863.[283] Due to the nature of his occupation, he was quickly called upon to leave Flint and relocate to other parts of Michigan. Smart continued preaching, and eventually ended up at Albion College, where he was awarded the degree of Doctor of Divinity. He remained active in the college for many years, and served as its trustee from 1868 until his death twenty-four years later.

---

[280] James Smart, *National Fast: A Fast Day Sermon*, 8.
[281] Ellis, 93.
[282] James Smart, letter in *Wolverine Citizen*, November 8, 1862.
[283] *Record of Service of Michigan Volunteers in the Civil War, 1861-1865, 23rd Michigan Infantry*, 95.

He died of a stroke on March 2, 1892, and his funeral was held at the Garland Street Church in Flint.[284] Smart was buried at Clinton Grove Cemetery in Clinton, Michigan.

John Hughes

John Hughes was born on November 16, 1842, the eighth child of Christopher and Mary Hughes. He grew up in Vienna Township of Clio. At age ten, his parents moved the family to Genesee Township, where they resided in the years leading up to the Civil War. In August 1862, Hughes enlisted in the 23rd Michigan Infantry, Company C. He fought as a soldier in the unit until the end of the war in 1865.[285] After the war, Hughes spent many years working as a clerk at a general store in Mount Morris, and became active in mercantile. In 1866, he married Emily Mann. Eventually, the couple moved to Evart, Michigan, where he worked as a carpenter and contractor. After nearly twenty years, Hughes returned to Mount Morris, where he took an interest in farming.

During his time in Genesee County, Hughes and his family contributed greatly to the community. He was a trustee in Mount Morris for several years. His father Christopher donated land on Saginaw Street for the construction of Saint Mary's Catholic Church, where John and his wife became dedicated parishioners. During their marriage, John and Emily had eight children, but four of them died at a young age.[286] Hughes spent the remainder of his life in Mount Morris, until his death in 1923. He is buried at Calvary Cemetery behind Saint Mary's Catholic Church, along with a number of other members of his family.

Richard H. Hughes

We are not in Atlanta yet, though by going a few steps from where I am writing, I can see the City. It is a pretty sight by night to see

---

[284] *Journal and Reports of the Thirty-Seventh Annual Session of the Detroit Conference of the Methodist Episcopal Church*, 58-59.
[285] *Biographical History of Genesee County*, 329.
[286] *Biographical History of Genesee County*, 329-333.

our bomb shells bursting over the City, as the shelling is kept up constantly.[287]

—Richard Hughes, 23rd Michigan Infantry

(An account of the Atlanta Campaign of 1864)

Richard Henry Hughes was born on January 9, 1840, in Oakland County. He was the son of William and Mary, who moved to a farm in Mount Morris when he was a child.[288] During the Civil War, he was a private in the 23rd Michigan Infantry, Co. K. As a soldier, Hughes fought primarily in the Western Theatre, and was frequently engaged in Tennessee and Georgia. Perhaps most notably, he was involved in the Atlanta Campaign of 1864. During the campaign, Hughes wrote to his father, saying:

> On the 22nd of this month, the rebs charged nearly the whole length of our line, and were repulsed with very heavy loss. Their papers state it at 10,000: while our loss did not exceed 4,000, though we lost Maj.-Gen McPherson. We got so near the City, we were throwing shells into town. This the rebels did not like, so they tried to drive us back, but did not succeed. A few more such charges from the rebels will use Johnston's army up. There were 1,000 rebels buried in front of one Division of the 15th Corps, besides the wounded. Probably you will never see such a sight. I was not exactly in the fight, but was within musket-shot of it. You may say—strange that our loss should be so much less than the rebels'. I will explain: they charged our breastworks with the intention of driving us back, out of range of the City, but failed in the attempt. We had every chance to mow them down as they advanced. The prisoners say they have longed to be captured, and appear to be quite happy in our hands, where they think they are safe. When we talk about exchanging them—they don't want to be exchanged: say they have fought long enough.[289]

---

[287] Richard Hughes, letter in *Wolverine Citizen*, August 13, 1864.
[288] Michigan Historical Commission, *Collections Report of the Pioneer Society of the State of Michigan* (Lansing: Wynkoop Hallenbeck Crawford Company, 1908), 35.
[289] Richard Hughes, letter in *Wolverine Citizen*, August 13, 1864.

Hughes survived the Civil War, and mustered out of service on May 29, 1865.[290] After the war, he returned to Mt. Morris, and married the daughter of R. W. Dullam in 1869. They had four children.[291] As a resident of Mt. Morris, Hughes played an active role in local politics. In 1874 and 1875, he was the Mt. Morris Township Clerk. In 1877, he was elected as the Supervisor of Mt. Morris Township.[292] Later in life, Hughes gave up work as a farmer. Instead, he built and operated an apple evaporating factory in Flint. He was also a deputy state oil inspector, and the first commander of the Crapo Post, G.A.R. He was active in a number of fraternal organizations, including the Genesee Commandery Knights Templar and the Ancient Order of United Workmen.[293]

As the deputy state oil inspector in 1866, Hughes went to Bay City on a business trip. During the journey, he became so ill that he was bedridden upon arrival. His wife quickly went to Bay City to be with him, and was by his side during his final moments. Hughes died on February 11, 1886. The funeral was held at the Court Street Methodist Church, and was officiated by Reverend I. N. Elwood.[294] Hughes was buried in Glenwood Cemetery.

30th MICHIGAN INFANTRY

The 30th Michigan Infantry mustered into service on January 9, 1865. The regiment was formed specifically to defend the borders of Michigan, because it was feared that Confederate sympathizers and refugees in Canada would raid cities and towns within the state. The 30th

---

[290] Ellis, 100.
[291] Michigan Historical Commission, *Collections Report of the Pioneer Society of the State of Michigan*, 35.
[292] Ellis, 316-317.
[293] Michigan Historical Commission, *Collections Report of the Pioneer Society of the State of Michigan*, 36.
[294] Michigan Historical Commission, *Collections Report of the Pioneer Society of the State of Michigan*, 35-36.

Michigan was never engaged in battle, but fifteen of its members died of disease. It was mustered out of service on June 30, 1865.[295]

William E. Christian

> We are passing through one of those eras that occur only once in a thousand years, when events are passing in which the destiny of the human race is involved. Things that have darkened the page of history through centuries of petty wars and revolution now find their parallel in this fresh rain of blood; and now we are to see whether the "Great Republic" will fall, or whether it shall live.[296]
>
> —William E. Christian, 8th and 30th Michigan Infantry

William E. Christian was born in Utica, New York, the son of George and Sarah Christian. While the exact date of his birth is unknown, marriage records indicate that he was married in September 1868 at the age of 30. Therefore, he must have been born in either 1837 or 1838.[297] Christian entered the military on August 12, 1861. He served as a Commissary Sergeant in the 8th Michigan Infantry, Co. G.[298] Christian was involved in quite a bit intense combat during his service, including a bloody affair the Battle of James Island. After the battle, he wrote:

> The slaughter was perfectly horrible. Many of our boys clambered into the fort and died fighting their gunners. Bravely they walked up to the breastworks, never wavering, never flinching, while the guns mowed them down in heaps. No sooner would one get inside than he would charge on the gunners, never looking back to see if his comrades were following him.[299]

---

[295] *Record of Service of Michigan Volunteers in the Civil War, 1861-1865, 30th Michigan Infantry*, 1-2.
[296] William E. Christian, letter in *Wolverine Citizen*, May 7, 1864.
[297] Familysearch.org, "William E. Christian, 1868 Michigan Marriages," https://familysearch.org/pal:/MM9.1.1/NQWV-M7M (accessed May 23, 2012).
[298] Robertson, 48 (of Volume III).
[299] William E. Christian, letter in *Wolverine Citizen*, July 5, 1862.

After serving with the 8th Michigan Infantry for three years, Christian left the regiment. He then enlisted as a Captain in the 30th Michigan Infantry on November 28, 1864. The regiment was formed specifically for the purpose of protecting Michigan's borders. After all, the growing number of southern refugees and rebel sympathizers in Canada created a large threat of an attack on Michigan itself. Christian stayed with the 30th Michigan for the remainder of the war and mustered out of the service on June 24, 1865.[300] After the war, he returned to Flint and married Maggie Cooley on September 30, 1868.[301] In the latter years of his life, the couple moved to Bay City and raised a family. Christian continued to reside there, working as an artist until his death on December 31, 1886.[302] He was buried in Pine Ridge Cemetery in Bay City, Michigan.[303] After his death, Maggie moved to Cleveland, Ohio, and remained there until she died on March 29, 1934.[304]

1st U. S. SHARPSHOOTERS

The 1st U. S. Sharpshooters was organized during the summer of 1861, and was commanded by Hiram Berdan. It joined the Army of the Potomac, and fought in every major battle of the Peninsula Campaign of 1862. Later that year, it was also engaged at Antietam and Fredericksburg. In 1863, the regiment fought at Chancellorsville, Gettysburg and Mine Run. The following year, it was at the Wilderness, Spotsylvania, Cold Harbor, and Petersburg. At the end of 1864, the soldiers' terms of enlistment had ended. Those who chose to reenlist were consolidated with the 2nd U. S. Sharpshooters, and remained with that regiment until it disbanded in February 1865.[305]

---

[300] Robertson, 48 (of Volume III).
[301] Familysearch.org, "William E. Christian, 1868 Michigan Marriages," https://familysearch.org/pal:/MM9.1.1/NQWV-M7M (accessed May 23, 2012).
[302] Familysearch.org, "William E. Christian, 1870 U.S. Census," https://familysearch.org/pal:/MM9.3.1/TH-266-11686-58577-2?cc=1438024 (accessed May 23, 2012).
[303] Sons of Union Veterans, "Graves Registration: Department of Michigan," http://www.suvcwmi.org/graves/search.php (accessed May 23, 2012).
[304] Familysearch.org, "Ohio Deaths, 1908-1953, Margaret L. Christian," https://familysearch.org/pal:/MM9.3.1/TH-1942-21322-22798-15?cc=1307272 (accessed May 23, 2012).
[305] Company C First United States Sharpshooters, a Civil War reenacting organization,

James B. Delbridge

I have been all over the field and saw hundreds lying dead, some torn to pieces and some with just a gun shot wound. A portion lay on the field three days. I saw them put thirty or forty together in a pit, others were buried singly. The enemy left their dead and wounded on the field. The wounded rebels were well taken care of. Among other sights, I witnessed a load of arms and legs buried, that had been amputated.[306]

—James B. Delbridge, 1st U. S. Sharpshooters

James B. Delbridge was born in Batavia, New York, on January 25, 1837. His father moved the family to Michigan shortly after it entered into statehood.[307] In the summer following the attack on Fort Sumter, Delbridge eagerly enlisted in the 1st U. S. Sharpshooters, Company C. As a soldier, he was not a stranger to battle. In one of his earliest combat experiences, he described a skirmish that took place with the rebel pickets, which resulted in one man being wounded in the leg and his finger shot off. When recalling the incident, Delbridge argued, "Our friends are mistaken about Sharp Shooters not being exposed as much as Infantry, for the woods are full of rebels. We are all very anxious to get the first shot at them, but I do not intend to rush wildly into danger, but stand my chance with the rest."[308]

Delbridge's most fearful moment came during the Peninsula Campaign of 1862. While in Mechanicsville, the Confederates mounted a surprise flank attack, which caused Delbridge and his companions to scatter, trying to avoid capture. Knowing that the enemy would show no quarter to sharpshooters, Delbridge later recalled:

"The US Sharpshooters and the Original Company C: a Brief History," *Company C First Regiment Berdan's Sharpshooters*, http://www.1stussharpshooters.com/oldcompanyc.html (accessed October 27, 2012).
[306] James B. Delbridge, letter in *Wolverine Citizen*, May 24, 1862.
[307] Paul Leake, *History of Detroit* (Chicago and New York: Lewis Publishing Company, 1912), 562.
[308] James B. Delbridge, letter in *Wolverine Citizen*, Oct. 5, 1861.

I started for the Chickahominy, hoping to make my escape by that way. I got where our Batteries were shelling the rebels' advancing forces, and was there taken and double quicked back to their reserve. I expected rifle-men would receive no quarter; and I can assure you my mind was troubled just then. I was taken to Gen. Jackson. He asked me what Regiment I belonged to. I told him to the First U. S., which was correct; but I left off the S. S. He then commenced questioning me about our forces, and how situated. I asked him if he thought I would give information, because I was a prisoner. He laughed and said, If I did he might not be able to rely on it. Some threw out abuse; when he gave orders to have any that should abuse prisoners, arrested.[309]

After his capture, Delbridge was sent to a prison camp on Belle Isle in Richmond, Virginia. During his time there, he saw the cruelty that prisoners of war (on both sides) faced. For instance, Delbridge recalled that on July 16, 1862, about 500 sick and wounded men were brought to the camp from a hospital in Richmond. Many of them had limbs amputated only days before, and were given no surgical attendance. According to Delbridge's account, it was common to see three to five men lying dead in the camp every morning, many of whom had starved to death. Often, the bodies were left in the camp for days before they were finally buried.[310] Some of the Richmond citizens took pity on the soldiers, or sometimes even tried to make a profit from them. As Delbridge later recalled, "I saw a woman dragged to the guard-house for selling pies to prisoners. She fought desperately, and it took three men to get her to the guard house."[311]

Luckily, the Confederates released Delbridge during a prisoner exchange. On August 6, 1862, he returned to the Union Army.[312] On February 6, 1863, he was discharged due to disability.[313] He returned to his wife, Ellen Jane (Fisher) Delbridge. The couple continued to reside in Michigan with their four children, where he engaged in the lumber

---

[309] James B. Delbridge, letter in *Wolverine Citizen*, September 27, 1862.
[310] James B. Delbridge, letter in *Wolverine Citizen*, September 27, 1862.
[311] James B. Delbridge, letter in *Wolverine Citizen*, September 27, 1862.
[312] M. A. Watson, "Release of James B. Delbridge," *Wolverine Citizen*, August 16, 1862.
[313] Ellis, 113.

business. They moved throughout the state, and eventually ended up in Detroit.[314] He died on August 1, 1907, and is buried in Woodlawn Cemetery in Detroit.[315]

Martin A. Watson

On Wednesday night the Colonel and Major of the 93d New York, deserted and went over to the rebels here. It is supposed that they conveyed considerable information to them, but it can't be very cheering to them if they tell the truth. The Colonel sent a flag of truce over for his horse and things; they sent word back that the rebel army must furnish him, if they wanted him: that Uncle Sam would take care of his things.[316]

—Martin A. Watson, 1st U. S. Sharpshooters

Martin A. Watson was born in 1841. As a young man, he enlisted in the 1st U. S. Sharpshooters shortly after the attack on Fort Sumter in 1861.[317] He wrote home frequently throughout the war, and his letters were often published in the *Wolverine Citizen*. In these letters, he often described encounters with a number of famous figures. On one occasion, Watson wrote about the regiment being visited by President Lincoln, who complimented the soldiers for their outstanding marksmanship.[318] In another letter, he mentioned that General McClellan passed by the regiment during one of the marches, which greatly raised the morale of the men in his unit. He praised McClellan, claiming, "I actually think if Gen. McClellan was to be removed from his command, that four-fifths of this army would throw down their arms and refuse to fight."[319] Like Delbridge, Watson emphasized the extreme danger that was associated with being a

---

[314] Leake, 562.
[315] Seekingmichigan.org, "Death Records, 1897-1920," seekingmichigan.org (accessed May 11, 2012).
[316] Martin A. Watson, letter in *Wolverine Citizen*, May 10, 1862.
[317] United States Department of Veterans Affairs, "National Gravesite Locator," http://gravelocator.cem.va.gov/j2ee/servlet/NGL_v1 (accessed May 8, 2012).
[318] Martin A. Watson, Letter in *Wolverine Citizen*, Oct. 5, 1861.
[319] Martin A. Watson, letter in *Wolverine Citizen*, May 24, 1862.

sharpshooter. Often, if a sharpshooter was captured in battle, they faced execution. Watson made this harsh reality very clear in a letter published by the *Wolverine Citizen* on May 24, 1862, when he attested:

> Gen. McGruder is down on us S. S. A deserter says he heard him say, that if he gets one of them S. S. he will hang him, and then quarter him, and cut him into inch pieces. He will see if he is going to have his men slaughtered in that way. The only advice I can give him is not to holloa until he is out of the woods; for it might so happen that he would run against one of those little bullets and thus end his career. Death at the hands of a S. S. is very quick and he would scarcely know it.[320]

Luckily for Watson, he avoided capture and survived the war. In January of 1864, he transferred into the Invalid Corps.[321] By war's end, he had risen to the rank of Corporal. Watson lived until 1901, and was buried in Arlington National Cemetery.[322]

4th MICHIGAN CAVALRY

The 4th Michigan Cavalry mustered into service on August 29, 1862, and was sent to Kentucky. Throughout most of 1862, its main objective was to confront and defeat Confederate cavalry under John Morgan. While in Kentucky, the regiment met Morgan's cavalrymen frequently, skirmishing against them at Stanford, Crab Orchard, Lebanon, and a number of other places.[323] In May of the following year, the 4th Michigan Cavalry charged three Confederate camps, taking fifty-five prisoners and routing the enemy. It fought and pursued Morgan's cavalry until it reached Chattanooga, Tennessee, where it was severely repulsed. In 1864, the regiment was a part of Sherman's campaign in Georgia. After the fall of Atlanta, it pursued and harassed Confederate forces in Tennessee under John Bell Hood. In 1865, the 4th Michigan Cavalry aided in the capture of Selma, Alabama, where it fought against Confederate

---

[320] Martin A. Watson, letter in *Wolverine Citizen*, May 24, 1862.
[321] Ellis, 113.
[322] United States Department of Veterans Affairs, "National Gravesite Locator."
[323] Ellis, 106.

cavalry under General Nathan Bedford Forrest. After Lee's surrender at Appomattox, the 4th Michigan Cavalry pursued Jefferson Davis, and was responsible for his capture on May 10, 1865. The regiment mustered out of service on July 1, 1865.[324]

George W. Fish

We captured a mail, with very important official information relating to the army—also all sorts of private correspondence. One ardent young Southern officer had written two declarations of love and proposals for marriage, to two different young ladies, sending both by the same mail. He professed himself near desperation—his love was so terribly *severe*, in both cases. Verily, this rebellion makes the "cavaliers" traitors, even in love: disloyal even to the fair sex.[325]

—George W. Fish, 4th Michigan Cavalry

George Whitefield Fish was born in Kortright, New York, on July 16, 1816. As a young man, he attended a university at Castleton, Vermont, where he graduated as a physician at the age of twenty-one. In 1838, he married Octavia Aldruda Mowra. The couple moved to Flint, Michigan, where Fish opened his medical practice. In 1859, he went on a voyage to China, but returned to the United States once the Civil War was underway.[326]

Fish enlisted as a surgeon in the 4th Michigan Cavalry on July 26, 1862.[327] His sons, George F. Fish and Delaski W. Fish, were also in the regiment. Less than a year after his enlistment, he was captured at the Battle of Stones River, but was released after a short time. After his release, Fish served with the regiment until the close of the war, and participated in more than fifty battles. As members of the 4th Michigan

---

[324] Ellis, 106.
[325] George W. Fish, letter in *Wolverine Citizen*, May 16, 1863.
[326] Michigan Historical Commission, *Michigan Historical Collections: Report of the Pioneer and Historical Society of the State of Michigan* (Lansing: Thorp and Godfrey, State Printers and Binders, 1886), 196-198.
[327] Ellis, 106.

Cavalry, he and his sons were present during the capture of Jefferson Davis in 1865.[328]

Fish was an ardent abolitionist, and his opposition to slavery was made very apparent in the letters he sent home. In a letter published by the *Wolverine Citizen* on April 23, 1864, he argued, "Nearly every man in this army has long since made up his mind that Slavery being the cause of the war, dies; and that hereafter an American citizen will not have to blush for his country because of Slavery."[329] Later, in the same letter, he wrote:

> Negro soldiers are becoming a power in the army; yesterday a fine Regiment passed our camp, on its way to the front, guarding a large wagon train. A finer looking set of men I have seldom seen, and their soldierly bearing received the cordial commendation of officers and men. As they marched by us, bearing proudly aloft the beautiful banner of our country, every soldier's heart felt warmed towards them, and manly voices bade them God speed. No fear of "Negro equality" here. It would be doing these loyal negroes gross injustice to call them equal with the miserable white traitors North or South, who are in sympathy with rebels.[330]

Fish mustered out of service on August 15, 1865. After the war, he returned to Flint, where he became a member of the Genesee County Medical Society.[331] He moved to California for a brief time, where he acted as manager of the Monitor Silver Mines until illness in his family caused him to return to Flint. In 1878, he was appointed by the federal government as Consul, and was sent to Tunis, Africa, where he lived for four years before returning home. He served as the Collector of Internal Revenue for Michigan's Sixth District for two years. He also spent time as editor of the *Saginaw Daily Enterprise*. Fish served as a state senator and as an alderman for the city of Flint. He was a trustee for the Michigan School for the Deaf, Dumb and Blind for six years. He was also one of the

---

[328] Michigan Historical Commission, *Michigan Historical Collections: Report of the Pioneer and Historical Society of the State of Michigan*, 198.
[329] George W. Fish, letter in *Wolverine Citizen*, April 23, 1864.
[330] George W. Fish, letter in *Wolverine Citizen*, April 23, 1864.
[331] Ellis, 57.

original organizers of the Methodist Church on Court Street, and served as its trustee, steward, treasurer, and Sunday school superintendent.[332]

Fish faced a large amount of tragedy in his life. While he was working for a coal mining company in California in 1874, his oldest daughter Julia became ill. He returned to Genesee County just in time to see her die of consumption. Less than a month later, his son George died of the same illness. A couple of years after their deaths, his wife Octavia died. He eventually remarried, this time to S. A. Rulison, whom he lived with for the remainder of his life. On September 6, 1885, his daughter Aldruda also died of consumption. Fish went out to Glenwood Cemetery to prepare her burial plot. While doing so, he came down with a cold, which quickly turned into pneumonia. On September 19, 1885, less than two weeks after his daughter's death, George W. Fish died at the age of 69. His funeral was held at Court Street Methodist Church, and he was buried with the rest of his family at Glenwood Cemetery. He was survived by his second wife, and his sons Delaski and Frank.[333]

George Raab

"War is an awful thing. People used to stand up and shoot each other and then chat back and forth when the shooting stopped. I hope the United States will never get into another war."[334]

—George Raab, 4th Michigan Cavalry

One of the most interesting accounts about the capture of Jefferson Davis came from George Raab of the 4th Michigan Cavalry. Raab was born on March 17, 1846, in Wetzlar, Germany. His parents, Eberhadt and Catherine Raab, moved to the United States when he was nine years old. At first, the family settled in New York, but it moved to Flint, Michigan,

---

[332] Michigan Historical Commission, *Michigan Historical Collections: Report of the Pioneer and Historical Society of the State of Michigan*, 197-201.
[333] Michigan Historical Commission, *Michigan Historical Collections: Report of the Pioneer and Historical Society of the State of Michigan*, 197-201.
[334] "Flint Man is Sole Survivor of Detachment which Captured Jeff Davis at Close of Civil War; Will be 89 in March," *Flint Journal*, February 10, 1935.

in 1858. At the age of fourteen, he began an apprenticeship under William Miller, who was a cabinet maker in the Flint area.[335]

At the age of seventeen, Raab ended his apprenticeship, and enlisted in the 4th Michigan Cavalry on January 5, 1864.[336] Among other engagements, he fought at Selma, Alabama, and Macon, Georgia.[337] He also played a major role in the capture of Jefferson Davis. Raab was never wounded during the war, but recalled that on one occasion a bullet came so close to him that it blistered his nose. Furthermore, he was thrown off his horse during the war, which resulted in a spine injury that afflicted him for the rest of his life.[338]

After the war, he returned to Flint and renewed his career as a cabinet maker. In 1867, he moved to Lawrence, Michigan, where he opened a furniture store. While living in Lawrence, he married Hattie E. Tomlinson. In 1871, the couple returned to Flint, and Raab assisted in the completion of the Michigan School for the Deaf, Dumb and Blind. A year later, he moved to Holly and opened another furniture store, but moved back to Flint after only a couple of years. After returning to Flint, he opened a grocery store, which burned down after only two years. Then, working with his younger brother Jacob, he opened a cabinet-making shop. In 1884, he partnered with Richard Hughes and opened another grocery store. Two years later, he sold his share of the store, and began working with sewing machines.[339] Raab and his wife had six children. He was an active member of the community, and served as the Supervisor of Flint's Fourth Ward for many years. He was a member of the Grand Army of the Republic and the National League of Veterans and Sons.[340]

---

[335] *Portrait and Biographical Record of Genesee, Lapeer and Tuscola Counties, Michigan*, 756.
[336] "Flint Man is Sole Survivor of Detachment which Captured Jeff Davis at Close of Civil War; Will be 89 in March," *Flint Journal*, February 10, 1935.
[337] *Portrait and Biographical Record of Genesee, Lapeer and Tuscola Counties, Michigan*, 757.
[338] "Flint Man is Sole Survivor of Detachment which Captured Jeff Davis at Close of Civil War; Will be 89 in March," *Flint Journal*, February 10, 1935.
[339] *Portrait and Biographical Record of Genesee, Lapeer and Tuscola Counties, Michigan*, 757.
[340] *Portrait and Biographical Record of Genesee, Lapeer and Tuscola Counties, Michigan*, 701, 704.

In February 1935, at the age of eighty-eight, Raab was interviewed by the *Flint Journal*. During the interview, he gave a vivid account about his involvement in the capture of Jefferson Davis. When recalling the event, which had taken place on May 10, 1865, Raab claimed,

> When we came up, Jeff Davis came out dressed in a long waterproof coat, with a woman's shawl over his head and a water pail over his arm. Mrs. Davis called to ask if her 'mother' could go to the spring to get some water, but as the Confederate president started, someone in the Union forces called out to Mrs. Davis, 'What in hell is your mother wearing spurs for?'[341]

During the capture of Jefferson Davis, Raab managed to take quite a few souvenirs that belonged to the Confederate president. He took a hand mirror and a hat that belonged to Davis. Not recognizing its historical significance, he threw the hat away after purchasing a new one only a short time later. Nonetheless, Raab kept the mirror in his possession. During the interview, he also noted that a soldier from Lapeer, Michigan, took a horse that belonged to Davis. The man brought the horse to Michigan, and on one occasion even rode it into Flint.[342]

Less than one month after the interview, Raab died. He was only days away from his eighty-ninth birthday, and was buried in Gracelawn Cemetery in Flint, Michigan.[343]

6th MICHIGAN CAVALRY

The 6th Michigan Cavalry mustered into service in October 1862, and contained nearly fifty men from Genesee County. In 1863, it joined the Army of the Potomac, and was promptly assigned to the "Michigan

---

[341] "Flint Man is Sole Survivor of Detachment which Captured Jeff Davis at Close of Civil War; Will be 89 in March," *Flint Journal*, February 10, 1935.
[342] "Flint Man is Sole Survivor of Detachment which Captured Jeff Davis at Close of Civil War; Will be 89 in March," *Flint Journal*, February 10, 1935.
[343] Sons of Union Veterans, Department of Michigan, *Graves Registration*, http://www.suvcwmi.org/graves/search.php (accessed January 15, 2012).

Cavalry Brigade" commanded by General George Armstrong Custer. In the summer of 1863, the regiment frequently skirmished with Confederates in Pennsylvania. Most notably, it fought at the Battle of Gettysburg on July 3, 1863.[344] By 1864, it was constantly on the move in Virginia, raiding towns and encountering Confederates on an almost weekly basis. In 1865, the 6th Michigan fought at such places as Five Forks, Sailor's Creek, and Appomattox, Virginia. At the end of the war, Confederate General George Pickett complimented a valiant assault made by the 6th Michigan Cavalry, saying that it was "the bravest charge that he had ever seen."[345] The regiment was present for Lee's surrender at Appomattox. Even though the war had ended, the 6th Michigan Cavalry was not given permission to muster out of service. Rather, it was sent westward to Indian country. Most of its members were finally mustered out of service in November 1865. The remaining soldiers were consolidated with the 1st Michigan Cavalry.[346]

James C. Parsons

He rode up to Gen. Custer and asked him about the condition of our troops. Custer replied that one Corps of Infantry, and the Cavalry, were all right yet, but the other two Corps were badly broken. Gen. Sheridan said: "Tonight Mrs. Sheridan is a widow, or we camp on the ground we left this morning." Wheeling his horse, he dashed down our lines and such a cheering you never heard.[347]

—James C. Parsons, 6th Michigan Cavalry

James C. Parsons was born in Grand Blanc on May 13, 1837. He was the son of Edward Parsons and Sarah Baldwin.[348] During the Civil War, he enlisted in the 6th Michigan Cavalry, Company I, a regiment

---

[344] Ellis, 109.
[345] Ellis, 109.
[346] Ellis, 109.
[347] James C. Parsons, letter in *Wolverine Citizen*, November 12, 1864.
[348] Seekingmichigan.org, "Death Records, 1897-1920," www.seekingmichigan.org (accessed May 18, 2012).

which served under Custer. Parsons, like many of his comrades, was very fond of Custer. When describing the "Boy General" he remembered:

> Many a hard fight have we been in with Custer at our head. Many a time has death or Libby Prison seemed inevitable, but Custer has led us through. Our men idolized him. He is a brave and great General. He was with Kilpatrick long enough to get much of his daring, dashing, dare-devil style, and at the same time possess that cool courage and great judgment, which the dashing Kilpatrick cannot boast of. [349]

As a cavalryman, Parsons was involved in a number of engagements. As stated in *Custer and His Wolverines: The Michigan Cavalry Brigade, 1861-1865* by Edward G. Longacre, Parsons was believed to have been involved in a dangerous shootout with Confederate General Wade Hampton in a skirmish that took place on the road to Gettysburg. According to Longacre, during the skirmish Hampton singled out a federal trooper to attack. The trooper, allegedly James Parsons, exchanged several shots with Hampton, until his rifle jammed. Parsons raised his hand, asking for a momentary pause to fix his weapon. Hampton, recognizing the unfairness of the situation, agreed. After fixing his weapon, the engagement resumed until Hampton shot Parsons in the wrist, causing him to retreat into a nearby forest.[350] After the incident preceding Gettysburg, Parsons participated in quite a few other engagements. Referring to another skirmish the following year, he wrote about a surprise attack by Mosby's raiders that took place on Thanksgiving Day of 1864. He stated:

> But Moseby, the noted guerilla chief, was hovering around and doubtless smelled our turkey. About noon, as we were preparing our dinner, Moseby, with 300 men made a dash on our pickets, three quarters of a mile out, and drove them in at full speed. They yelled like a lot of demons. The order—"To Horse!" was instantly given, and as instantly changed "To carbine and fall into line." So into line we fell, every man with the "old seven-shooter" up to his shoulder. On the "gray devils" came, across the broad field, right on the heels of the pickets. The order "Forward!" was given, and our whole Regiment moved forward at a sharp double-quick. We

---

[349] James C. Parsons, letter in *Wolverine Citizen*, April 8, 1865.
[350] Edward G. Longacre, *Custer and His Wolverines: The Michigan Cavalry Brigade, 1861-1865* (Cambridge, MA: Da Capo Press, 2004), 140.

were coming together fast, and in a few moments more we expected a lively old time. But Moseby could not stand our looks, and away he dashed.[351]

Parsons was mustered out of service on November 24, 1865.[352] In 1899, he married Nellie K. Wines.[353] The couple moved to Marion Township of Livingston County, where he took up farming. He resided there until his death on March 24, 1920.[354] He is buried in Evergreen Cemetery in Grand Blanc.

The Aplin Brothers

In the opening stages of the Civil War, three Aplin brothers from Genesee County, George, Henry and Tommy, promptly enlisted to fight for the Union. They came from an unhappy household, and animosity within the family eventually resulted in the separation of their parents, Thomas and Elvira.[355] During the war, the boys wrote home frequently to their mother and to their sisters Sarah and Mary, who were residents of Flint.[356]

Before the war, the oldest Aplin son, George, had been a teacher.[357] However, he quickly gave up the occupation and enlisted as a Sergeant in the 10th Michigan Infantry, Company I, on October 23, 1861, at the age of twenty-three.[358] During the war, he fought mainly on the western front,

---

[351] James C. Parsons, letter in *Wolverine Citizen*, December 17, 1864.
[352] Ellis, 109.
[353] "Marriage Records," *Livingston County Marriage Index*, http://www.memoriallibrary.com/MI/Livingston/Wed/wiltor.htm (accessed May 18, 2012).
[354] Seekingmichigan.org, "Death Records, 1897-1920," www.seekingmichigan.org (accessed May 18, 2012).
[355] "Aplin family papers, finding aid," William L. Clements Library, The University of Michigan, http://quod.lib.umich.edu/c/clementsmss/umich-wcl-M-2380apl?view=text (accessed June 5, 2012).
[356] Mary was often given the nickname "Helen."
[357] "Aplin family papers, finding aid".
[358] *Record of Service of Michigan Volunteers in the Civil War, 1861-1865* (Kalamazoo, MI: Ihling Bros. & Everard), 7.

and was engaged at such places as Corinth, Mississippi, and Buzzard's Roost, Georgia. He also took part in Sherman's March to the Sea. George survived the war, and was discharged as a 1st Lieutenant in 1865.[359] He returned to Genesee County, where he married Ellen Johnson in 1866.[360] The couple resided in Clio, and had numerous children.[361] He was elected as a school inspector for Thetford Township in 1867 and an inspector for Vienna Township in 1873.[362] George spent the remainder of his life in poverty. He attempted farming, but failed. Debt piled up and eventually forced foreclosure on his property. He then turned to his brother Henry, who was a prominent politician, for help. After pulling some strings, Henry was able to get his brother a political patronage appointment.[363] Because of this, George and Ellen moved away from Genesee County and took up residence in Cass City. George died in 1923, and was buried with his wife in Mount Morris Cemetery.

The second Aplin son, Henry,[364] was born on April 15, 1841, in Thetford Township. In 1848, his family moved to Flint, where he attended school and worked on the farm. On July 3, 1861, he enlisted in the 16th Michigan Infantry, Company C, and participated in a number of notable engagements as a soldier.[365] On July 30, 1862, he was captured at Savage Station, Virginia, and spent the next several months as a prisoner until he was exchanged later that year.[366] A few months after Henry's return to the 16th Michigan, he had the opportunity to see President Lincoln during a review of the Army. Henry later recalled, "Today the whole Army was out on review making over 100,000 soldiers in all in a haddy as close as they could be formed. I tell you it was a grand sight to see. . . Old Abe looked as natural as ever the boys cheard him long and loud as he rode past Regt. after Regt."[367] Henry's regiment participated in engagements at such

---

[359] *Record of Service of Michigan Volunteers in the Civil War, 1861-1865* (Kalamazoo, MI: Ihling Bros. & Everard), 7.
[360] Familysearch.org, "Michigan Marriages, 1822-1995," https://familysearch.org/pal:/MM9.1.1/FC6H-YY7 (accessed May 29, 2012).
[361] Familysearch.org, "United States Census, 1870," https://familysearch.org/pal:/MM9.3.1/TH-266-11686-63864-83?cc=1438024 (accessed June 5, 2012).
[362] Ellis, 372; 387.
[363] "Aplin family papers, finding aid".
[364] Henry was often given the nickname "Tip."
[365] "Henry Harrison Aplin," *Bay Journal*, http://bay-journal.com/bay/1he/writings/mibio-aplin-henry-h.html (accessed June 6, 2012).
[366] "Aplin family papers, finding aid".

places as Fredericksburg, Chancellorsville and Petersburg. Perhaps most significant was its involvement in the defense of Little Round Top at Gettysburg on July 2, 1863. Henry survived the war without receiving a single wound.[368]

After the war, Henry moved to Bay City, where he became active in the mercantile business. In 1879, he married Frances L. Patchen, and they later had a daughter, Daisy. He served as postmaster of West Bay City from 1869 to 1886, and again in 1898. Henry was elected as Auditor General of the Michigan in both 1886 and 1888. At the end of his term, he became general manager of an electric street railway in Bay City until 1891. As a devout Republican, he was elected as a representative in the State Legislature, and also served as a representative in the United States Congress in 1901.[369] During his life, Henry held positions as township clerk and treasurer, and was Chairman of the 10th district Republican Congressional Committee.[370] He died at his home in Bay City on July 23, 1910, and was buried in Elm Lawn Cemetery in Bay City. Aplin Beach in Bay County was named in his honor.[371]

The youngest of the three brothers was Arthur Aplin, who was given the nickname "Tommy." As a teenager, Tommy Aplin ran away from home to escape his troubled family life.[372] In July 1861, he enlisted in the 35th Illinois Infantry, Company D, under the name Thomas Arthur.[373] He was wounded at Pea Ridge, Arkansas in 1862. After recovering from his wound, he was engaged at Perryville, Kentucky, and Stone's River, Tennessee. In July 1863, he was placed on guard duty at a convalescent camp near Murfreesboro, Tennessee. After spending several months on guard duty, he requested to return to the fighting and was sent to the front in March 1864.[374] Tommy returned to his regiment in time to participate

---

[367] Henry Aplin, Letter from April 8, 1863, *Aplin Family Papers* (Ann Arbor: William L. Clements Library, University of Michigan).
[368] "Aplin family papers, finding aid".
[369] "Henry Harrison Aplin," *Bay Journal*.
[370] "Aplin family papers, finding aid".
[371] Henry Harrison Aplin," *Bay Journal*.
[372] "Aplin family papers, finding aid".
[373] "Illinois Civil War Detail Report," *Illinois State Archives*, http://www.ilsos.gov/isaveterans/civilMusterSearch.do?key=6701 (accessed June 7, 2012).
[374] "Aplin family papers, finding aid".

in Sherman's campaign through Georgia, and in a letter written to his mother, he stated:

> I am now a Color Guard—the post of honor, which is always also the post of danger. Our Colors have forty-nine holes through them, and one shot out the staff about half off. One Color Guard has been killed and another wounded.[375]

When reading the letter, it seems as though Tommy had premonitions about being wounded or killed in action. This prediction proved quite accurate, as he was wounded soon after the letter was written. Due to complications, he died in a military hospital on July 10, 1864, at the age of twenty.[376] He was buried in Glenwood Cemetery.

POSTWAR SOCIETIES

After returning home, the soldiers from Genesee County continued to be united by the powerful bonds that they had made during the war. Each regiment held reunions annually, many of which took place in the Flint area. Furthermore, a number of clubs and societies became popular in Genesee County. For instance, the Order of the Stars and Stripes, led by George Newall, consisted of over 100 local veterans. Another organization, Soldiers and Sailors of Genesee County, became prominent in 1879.[377] In December 1902, a branch of the National League of Veterans and Sons was formed in Flint, titled Camp William McKinley. It contained over 100 veterans from the area. One member from Flint, M. C. Barney, served as lieutenant-general of the organization at the national level.[378] These organizations were overshadowed by the Governor Crapo Post of the Grand Army of the Republic, which was founded in Flint in 1883. It was first commanded by Richard Hughes, and consisted of over 350 members at its peak.[379] After the Crapo Post was founded, a number

---

[375] Tommy Aplin, Letter in *Wolverine Citizen*, July 30, 1864.
[376] "Illinois Civil War Detail Report," *Illinois State Archives*.
[377] Wood, 698-699.
[378] Wood, 704.

of other posts sprung up in the communities surrounding Flint. A few of these included: the James Bradley Post in Clio, the Ransom Post in Flushing, the Henry W. Knapp Post in Davison, the Colonel Fenton Post in Fenton, and the Fred W. Walker Post in Mt. Morris.[380] Genesee County men continued to answer the call of duty even after the Civil War. In 1872, the Flint Union Blues was founded, which contained a significant number of Civil War veterans. The organization served as an active military company in Flint, and fought honorably during the Spanish-American War.[381]

Genesee County women also did their part to honor the Union veterans. In 1884, the Governor Crapo Relief Corps was organized in Flint. At times, its membership exceeded 100 people. This organization provided financial support for veterans, cared for the sick, assisted in burials, and helped decorate the graves of deceased veterans from the area.[382]

CONCLUSION

After examining the lives of these soldiers and their roles in the community, it is quite clear that Genesee County had a large impact on Michigan's role in the Civil War. Flint and its surrounding communities provided a number of regimental officers such as Stockton, Fenton and McCreery. These men were not only influential through their financial contributions and recruitment efforts, but also played a crucial role in Michigan's involvement in the war by setting an example of discipline and bravery for the men who fought under them. Furthermore, Genesee County offered a variety of other talents and resources to the Union Army. It provided Sarah Edmonds, who was the only woman ever fully accepted into the Grand Army of the Republic. It also contributed musicians such as Foote and Gardner, who coordinated the movement of entire regiments in the midst of battle by faithfully drumming the commands of their officers for the entire line to hear. Above all, it offered men of courage and

---

[379] Wood, 699-703.
[380] James T. Lyons, "Post Charters on File," *Sons of Union Veterans*, http://www.suvcwmi.org/gar/charters.pdf (accessed April 20, 2012).
[381] Wood, 705-708.
[382] Wood, 703-704.

dedication, as represented through Graham's valiant defense on Little Round Top and Ransom's selflessness at Second Manassas.

Likewise, the Civil War had a significant effect on the development of Genesee County and its culture. The war put local leaders like Fenton and McCreery in the spotlight, and made the rest of Michigan aware of their many successes. Fenton ran for Michigan state governor in the years following the war. Although his efforts to win the position proved unsuccessful, the Civil War nonetheless put him in the spotlight and made him a prominent political figure in Michigan. Had Fenton not commanded the 8th Michigan, he may not have achieved enough exposure to have even made it worth running for the position. Likewise, McCreery's escape from Libby Prison transformed him into a wartime hero. Because of this sudden growth in popularity, he had the opportunity to hold a number of political positions at both the state and national levels. These positions included State Treasurer, Collector of Internal Revenue, and United States Consul. By shaping these local figures into pronounced military heroes, the Civil War gave them the popularity that they needed to campaign for government positions. If the war had not occurred, people in other parts of the state may not have even known that these men existed. Therefore, the Civil War indirectly gave Genesee County a larger voice in Michigan politics. Furthermore, the war enriched the heritage of the County by helping the Flint area establish a sense of self-identity. Veterans like McCreery, Graham, Edmonds and Foote published accounts of their experiences in the Civil War for the rest of the nation to read. These writings made Genesee County aware of the rich, unique stories of its own local veterans. Because of this newfound awareness, a sense of pride developed in the area as a result of the war.

This pride remains a significant part of Genesee County even to this day. The Stockton Center frequently provides tours of the house, which has been turned into a museum. Each month, the local Sons of Union Veterans post, Governor Henry H. Crapo Camp No. 145, meets in an attempt to honor Civil War veterans and their accomplishments. Among other things, the group is dedicated to restoring vandalized or dilapidated headstones, participating in Memorial Day ceremonies and speaking at local schools about Civil War soldiers from the area. Similarly, a number of Mid-Michigan Civil War reenacting groups, including the 8th Michigan Medical and 14th Michigan Infantry, have developed in recent decades. These units participate in annual reenactments, which have previously been held at Genesee County locations such as Crossroads Village, Wolcott Orchards in Mount Morris and Almar Orchards in Flushing. Likewise, the Grand Blanc Living Historians Society frequently sets up Civil War encampments, and its members portray the daily lifestyles of both men and women of the period. By recognizing these groups and their contributions, it becomes certain that there are still many people who have dedicated themselves to sparking interest about the Civil War in their own neighborhoods.

As human beings, we often tend to distance ourselves from the things we read. These soldiers become almost surreal, and we often feel disconnected from them. It is important, however, to remember that these veterans are more than just characters in a story. They walked in our streets, prayed in our churches and lived in our neighborhoods. One soldier particularly drove this point home for me. While researching Genesee County Civil War veterans, I came across John Hughes. He was from Vienna Township of Clio, where I have lived my entire life. His father donated the land for the construction of Saint Mary's Catholic Church in Mount Morris. I attended school there from kindergarten through eighth grade, and I am still a parishioner there. He is buried in the cemetery behind the church, only a few yards from where I used to play during recess. Just like the connections I found between myself and Hughes, there are signs of these soldiers and their legacies in each of our daily lives. We just need take the time to notice them. The next time you are walking through downtown Flint, take a moment to imagine hundreds of men in blue parading down Saginaw Street. Or the next time you are near Burton, take a few minutes to stop by the For-Mar Nature Preserve and see the Foote Bird Museum. Remember these Genesee County soldiers. Learn not just their names, but their stories. It is the best way to honor them.

In closing, I felt it appropriate to add a poem written by Mrs. O. C. Gorton, a resident of Flint during the Civil War. Her words, which were written in 1864, eloquently describe the sacrifices of Genesee County's brave Civil War soldiers in a manner that greatly surpasses my own capability. It was published in the *Wolverine Citizen* on September 10, 1864, and reads:

The Soldier's Last Wish

O, would that I might once more look
    Upon the dear old flag,
That floats to-day where once was strung
    A hated rebel rag.
'Twas not an Ellsworth's hand that placed
    It there to proudly wave;
But it was one who risked as much,
    Whose heart was just as brave.

Comrades, my eyes are growing dim,
    And I can scarcely see;
It is but little more, kind ones,
    That you can do for me.
But will you bear me to some spot,
    Where I may see again
The flag that I have loved so much;
    Methinks 'twill ease this pain.

They gently bore his bleeding form
    From where he nobly fell,
And placed him where his eyes could rest
    On the flag he loved so well.
And when the sun's last rays fell on
    The glorious "Stripes and Stars,"
His soul had passed into that land
    Where there are no more wars.[383]

Genesee County contributed over 2,500 men to the war effort. Many of these men returned home after the Civil War and greatly helped shape the development of the area. It is important that we remember these soldiers and the impacts that they made in our own communities. However, a significant number of men from the Flint area never made it home from the war, and we must not forget them either. As descendants of these veterans and as beneficiaries of the contributions that they made, it is

---

[383] Colonel Elmer Ellsworth was shot while taking down a Confederate flag that flew over Alexandria, Virginia, in May 1861. He is considered to be one of the first martyrs for the Union cause; O. C. Gorton, poem in *Wolverine Citizen*, September 10, 1864.

our duty to tell their stories so that future generations may know of their significance. Otherwise, the legacy of these soldiers will be forever lost to time, and with it will go a substantial portion of our own heritage and history.

Bibliography

Libraries and Archives

Bentley Historical Library, University of Michigan, Ann Arbor, MI.

William L. Clements Library, University of Michigan, Ann Arbor, MI.

University of Michigan-Flint Archives, Flint, MI.

Primary Sources

Aplin family papers, William L. Clements Library, The University of Michigan.

Clarke Historical Library at Michiganinletters.org. "Sarah Emma Edmonds Seelye." Letter from Sarah Edmonds to Richard Halsted, dated September 6, 1897. Mount Pleasant: Clarke Historical Library, Central Michigan University. http://www.michiganinletters.org/2009/07/sarah-emma-edmonds-seelye_17.html (accessed May 31, 2012).

Colonel Stockton's Civil War Diary, Genesee Historical Collections Center at the University of Michigan-Flint, Flint, MI.

Diary of De Witt Spaulding. De Witt Spaulding Papers, Bentley Historical Library, University of Michigan.

Diary of William M. Fenton, 8th Michigan Infantry. McCreery-Fenton Family Papers [Microform, Roll 1], Bentley Historical Library, University of Michigan.

Edmonds, Sarah Emma. *Memoirs of a Soldier, Nurse and Spy: A Woman's Adventures in the Union Army*. DeKalb: Northern Illinois University Press, 1999.

Farewell Address of March 1863. McCreery-Fenton Family Papers [Microform, Roll 1], Bentley Historical Library, University of Michigan.

Flint Journal, 1919, 1935, 1944

Flushing Observer, 1901

Foote, Corydon Edward, and Olive Deane Hormel. *With Sherman to the Sea; A Drummer Boy's Story of the Civil War, as Related by Corydon Edward Foote to Olive Deane Hormel*. Ann Arbor: University of Michigan, 1960.

Fox, Wells B. *What I Remember of the Great Rebellion*. Lansing: Darius D. Thorp, Printer and Binder, 1892.

Genesee Democrat, 1861-65

"Glen-Wood Cemetery, The Fenton-McCreery Monument." *Wolverine Citizen, October 10,1885*. Mcreery-Fenton Family Papers [Microform, Roll 2], Bentley Historical Library, University of Michigan.

Graham, Ziba B.
On to Gettysburg. Ten Days from My Diary of 1863. Detroit: Winn & Hammond, Printers, 1893.

Ide, Alonzo C. "Diary of 1864." *United States Civil War Collection at Western Michigan University*. http://quod.lib.umich.edu/c/civilwar1/USCW006.0001.001/1:135?rgn=div1;view=fulltext (accessed May 29, 2012).

Jerome John Robbins Papers [Microform, Roll 1], Bentley Historical Library, University of Michigan.

McCreery-Fenton Family Papers, Bentley Historical Library, University of Michigan.

McCreery, William B. *My Experience as a Prisoner of War and Escape from Libby Prison*. Detroit: Winn & Hammond, 1893.

"Presentation of Civil War Flags to the State, July 4, 1866." *Rally Round the Flags*. Michigan Historical Museum.

http://www.hal.state.mi.us/mhc/museum/explore/museums/hismus/special/flags/flag1866.html (accessed January 16, 2012).

Record of Service of Michigan Volunteers in the Civil War, 1861-1865. Kalamazoo, MI: Ihling Bros. & Everard.

Smart, James. *National Fast: A Fast Day Sermon.* Flint: William Stevenson, Publisher, 1861.

Wolverine Citizen, 1861-65, 1871, 1885, 1896

Secondary Sources

"Aplin family papers, finding aid." William L. Clements Library, The University of Michigan. http://quod.lib.umich.edu/c/clementsmss/umich-wcl-M-2380apl?view=text (accessed June 5, 2012).

Archives of Michigan at *Seekingmichigan.org*. "Death Records, 1897-1920." www.seekingmichigan.org/discover/death-records.

Beyer, W. F. and O. F. Keydel. *Deeds of Valor; How America's Civil War Heroes Won the Congressional Medal of Honor.* Detroit, MI: Perrien-Keydel Co., 1903 (republished in Stamford, CT: Longmeadow Press, 1994).

Biographical History of Genesee County. Indianapolis: B. F. Bowen & Co., 1908.

Blum, Albert A. and Dan Geogakas. *Michigan Labor and the Civil* War. Lansing: Michigan Civil War Centennial Observance Commission, 1964.

Congressional Medal of Honor Society. "Clute, George W." *Congressional Medal of Honor Recipients.* http://www.cmohs.org/recipient-detail/266/clute-george-w.php (accessed February 9, 2012).

Cutler, William G. *History of the State of Kansas* (Chicago: A. T. Andreas, 1883). http://www.kancoll.org/books/cutler/labette/labette-co-p21.html (accessed June 14, 2012).

Dunbar, Willis F. *Michigan: A History of the Wolverine State*. Grand Rapids: William B. Eerdmans Publishing Company, 1970.

Ellis, Franklin. *History of Genesee County, Michigan*. Philadelphia: Everts & Abbott, 1879 publication. http://books.google.com/books?id=KxgVAAAAYAAJ&pg=PA9&source=gbs_toc_r&cad=4#v=onepage&q&f=false (accessed January 15, 2012).

Fenton Historical Society. "William M. Fenton." http://fentonhistsoc.tripod.com/id77.html (accessed February 15, 2012).

Flint Genealogical Society.
"Genesee County Death Index." http://www.rootsweb.ancestry.com/~mifgs/rbindex/wint-wooc_1.html (accessed June 27, 2012).

"Genesee County Marriage Index to 1934." http://www.rootsweb.ancestry.com/~mifgs/marriages/faaa-fazz_1.html (accessed May 29, 2012).

Gansler, Laura Leedy. *The Mysterious Private Thompson: The Double Life of Sarah Emma Edmonds, Civil War Soldier*. New York: A Division of Simon & Schuster, Inc., 2005.

Bingham, Stephen D. *Early History of Michigan*. Lansing: Thorp and Godfrey Printers and Binders, 1888.

Gray, Eugene F.

"Emma Nevada." *Michigan State University*. https://www.msu.edu/~graye/emma/chronolo.html (accessed April 23, 2012).

"Isaac Wixom Biography." *Michigan State University*. https://www.msu.edu/~graye/emma/IWixomBio.html (accessed April 23, 2012).

Green-Wood Cemetery, "Burial Search," http://www.green-wood.com/burial_results/index.php (accessed May 29, 2012).

Harvey, Don and Lois of http://www.michiganinthewar.org/.

Havrilcsak, Gregory M. "Thomas Baylis Whitmarsh Stockton: A Brief Talk." A speech presented during the dedication of the Michigan Historical Marker for the Stockton Home, 2005. Unpublished manuscript in possession of author.

Henderson, Don C. *The Red Book for the Thirtieth Legislature of the State of Michigan*. Lansing: W. S. George & Co., 1879.

"Henry Harrison Aplin," *Bay Journal*, http://bay-journal.com/bay/1he/writings/mibio-aplin-henry-h.html (accessed June 6, 2012).

Henry Howland Crapo Family Papers, Finding Aid. Genesee Historical Collections Center at Thompson Library, University of Michigan-Flint. http://www.umflint.edu/library/archives/crapo.htm (accessed May 17, 2012).

Hewes, Fletcher Willis. *History of the Formation, Movements, Camps, Scouts and Battles of the Tenth Regiment Michigan Volunteer Infantry*. Detroit: John Slater's Book and Job Printing Establishment, 1864.

"History of Fenton." *City of Fenton Official Website*. http://www.cityoffenton.org/pages/History-Of-Fenton/1 (accessed February 15, 2012).

"Illinois Civil War Detail Report." *Illinois State Archives*. http://www.ilsos.gov/isaveterans/civilMusterSearch.do?key=6701 (accessed June 7, 2012).

Jones, J. W. *The Story of American Heroism: Thrilling Narratives of Personal Adventures during the Great Civil War*. Akron, Ohio: The Werner Company, 1896.

Journal and Reports of the Thirty-Seventh Annual Session of the Detroit Conference of the Methodist Episcopal Church. Detroit: Wm. Graham Printing Co., 1892.

Leake, Paul. *History of Detroit*. Chicago and New York: Lewis Publishing Company, 1912.

Longacre, Edward G. *Custer and His Wolverines: The Michigan Cavalry Brigade, 1861-1865*. Cambridge, MA: Da Capo Press, 2004.

Lyons, James T. "Another Hall Found." *Newsletter of the Department of Michigan Sons of Union Veterans, summer 2004.* http://www.suvcwmi.org/gar/charters.pdf (accessed April 20, 2012).

"Marriage Records," *Livingston County Marriage Index*. http://www.memoriallibrary.com/MI/Livingston/Wed/wiltor.htm (accessed May 18, 2012).

McMullen, Dennis. *Colonel T. B. W. Stockton: Soldier, Engineer, Businessman*. Flint, Michigan: University of Michigan-Flint Archives, 1988.

"Michigan, Deaths, 1867-1897," index and images. *FamilySearch*. https://familysearch.org/pal:/MM9.1.1/N36N-6ZG : (accessed 31 May 2012), John E. Halsted, 03 Mar 1873.

Michigan Department of Natural Resources. "The Drummer Boy—A Poetry Lesson Plan." http://www.michigan.gov/dnr/0,4570,7-153-54463_18670_18793-52914--,00.html (accessed January 8, 2012).

Michigan Historical Commission.
    Collections Report of the Pioneer Society of the State of Michigan. Lansing: Wynkoop Hallenbeck Crawford Company, 1908.

Michigan Historical Collections: Report of the Pioneer and Historical Society of the State of Michigan. Lansing: Thorp and Godfrey, State Printers and Binders, 1886.

Milton Marion Fenner. http://www.civilwarsignals.org/brown/signalmen/248/miltonmfenner.pdf (accessed June 8, 2012).

Missouri State Archives. "Rachel v. William Walker (1836)". *Before Dred Scott: Freedom Suits in Antebellum Missouri.* http://www.sos.mo.gov/archives/education/aahi/beforedredscott/rachelV.asp (accessed January 22, 2012).

M. M. Fenner Hose Co. #2. http://www.fredoniafire.org/index_files/Page322.htm (accessed June 8, 2012).

Moore, Charles. *History of Michigan.* Chicago: The Lewis Publishing Company, 1915.

Moore, Frank. *The Civil War in Song and Story, 1860-1865.* P. F. Collier, Publisher, 1869.

"Oakwood Cemetery of Fenton, Genesee County, Tombstone Photographs." *U.S. Gen Web Archives Project.* http://www.usgwarchives.net/mi/tsphoto/genesee/oakwoodfenton/oakwoodfenton_s.htm (accessed August 7, 2012).

Portrait and Biographical Record of Genesee, Lapeer and Tuscola Counties, Michigan. Chicago: Chapman Bros., 1892.

The Profile of Milton M. Fenner from the 1881 Atlas of Chautauqua County. http://app.co.chautauqua.ny.us/hist_struct/Pomfret/Fenner_Milton-Profile.html (accessed June 8, 2012).

Robere, Bruce. "Colonel William B. McCreery: Commander, 21st Michigan Vol. Inf." *21st Michigan Volunteer Infantry.* http://www.21stmichigan.us/mccreery.htm (accessed January 8, 2012).

Robertson, John. Michigan Adjutant-General's Department. *Michigan in the War*. Lansing: W. S. George and Co., 1882.

Silliman, Sue Imogene. *Michigan Military Records*. Lansing: Michigan Historical Commission, 1920.

Sons of Union Veterans, Department of Michigan. *Graves Registration*. http://www.suvcwmi.org/graves/search.php (accessed January 15, 2012).

The Stockton Center at Spring Grove. "Thomas and Maria Stockton." http://stocktoncenter.org/Thomas&Maria/index.html (accessed January 22, 2012).

"United States Census, 1850," index and images. *FamilySearch*. https://familysearch.org/pal:/MM9.1.1/MF8D-2YH : (accessed 29 May 2012). Ellen Miles in household of Nathaniel M Miles, Flint, Genesee, Michigan, United States; citing dwelling 34, family 34, NARA microfilm publication M432, roll 350.

"United States Census, 1880," index and images. *FamilySearch*. https://familysearch.org/pal:/MM9.1.1/MWS7-J58 : (accessed 19 Jan 2013). John Willett in household of Geo. W. Oakes, Flint, Genesee, Michigan, United States; citing sheet 167A, family 2, NARA microfilm publication T9-0579.

"United States Census, 1900," index and images. *FamilySearch*. https://familysearch.org/pal:/MM9.1.1/MSM2-6WF : (accessed 31 May 2012). Richard H Halsted, ED 3 Concord township Concord village, Jackson, Michigan, United States; citing sheet 1A, family 8, NARA microfilm publication T623, FHL microfilm 1240719.

United States Department of Veterans Affairs. "National Gravesite Locator." http://gravelocator.cem.va.gov/j2ee/servlet/NGL_v1 (accessed May 8, 2012).

Wood, Edwin O. *History of Genesee County, Michigan: her People, Industries and Institutions*. Indianapolis: Federal Publishing Company, 1916.

Woodmere Cemetery. "Woodmere Cemetery Records Database."
    http://www.woodmerecemeteryresearch.com/records.php
    (accessed August 7, 2012).

Made in the USA
Lexington, KY
03 December 2013